THE PARANORMAL BOY

Jay Alani is one of India's leading paranormal investigators, with over 15 years of experience and more than 1,500 investigations across the world. A filmmaker, podcaster, author and TEDx speaker, he is known for his fearless pursuit of evidence-based paranormal inquiry and for pioneering India's only paranormal awareness helpline. His hit podcast *Paranormal Reality* has crossed 20 million streams and ranks among the top international horror shows.

Jay is the founder of The Paranormal Company, India's first paranormal startup, where he is building a global 'Paranormal Universe' through films, immersive storytelling, and technology. His upcoming projects—including *Winston Villa*, *The Paranormal Boy*, *Numinous*, and *Monster Café*—aim to reinvent Indian horror with authenticity and psychological depth.

His debut book *Haunted* (Penguin, 2019), India's first non-fiction horror title, received critical acclaim. Jay has secured multiple film deals based on his investigations and continues to create influential content with platforms such as Gaana, Dish TV, Pratilipi, and Brut India.

His work can be found on:
https://www.instagram.com/ijayalani
http://x.com/ijayalani

Prasun Roy is a bestselling author known for his accessible narrative style across genres including horror, crime thrillers, mythology, history and the paranormal. A researcher of India's unsung freedom fighters, his acclaimed work on Rash Behari Bose highlights significant INA contributions. He has also translated classics by Rabindranath Tagore and Bibhutibhushan Bandyopadhyay for global readers. A heritage enthusiast, Prasun serves as Convenor of Indian History Awareness and Research (IHAR) and is a life member of Indian National Trust for Art and Cultural Heritage (INTACH).

He has been a prominent speaker at many prestigious literary festivals, including Tata Steel Kolkata Literary Meet, Apeejay Kolkata Literary Festival, and Pune International Literary Festival, among others.

An alumnus of IIM Lucknow, he lives in Kolkata and manages his family's pharmaceutical business headquartered in Vadodara and Kolkata.

THE PARANORMAL BOY

The Journey of a Crusader

JAY ALANI
with
PRASUN ROY

RUPA

Published by
Rupa Publications India Pvt. Ltd 2026
161-B/4, Gulmohar House,
Yusuf Sarai Community Centre,
New Delhi 110049

Sales centres
Bengaluru Chennai
Hyderabad Kolkata Mumbai

P-ISBN: 978-93-6156-878-7
E-ISBN: 978-93-6156-995-1

First impression 2026

10 9 8 7 6 5 4 3 2 1

Printed in India

Dedicated to all the unsung crusaders of India who work fearlessly to eradicate blind faith from our society.

Contents

1

Superpower

Being different is a 'Power'.
Being 'Invisible' is a 'Superpower'.

1 January 2015, Patna, 02.45 a.m.

The Armageddon

'Wake up, Jay, time's up! This is the moment of ultimate disaster...'

'Who are you?' I asked as I opened my eyes. My room was empty and a thick darkness had coagulated around every corner. I failed to see anything, but the heavy male voice had a ruthlessness that froze the blood within my veins.

I knew I was alone in my room. The door was locked from inside. Then who was speaking to me? The winter night was chilly, but my whole body perspired with an unknown anxiety.

The voice screamed again, 'Who do you think you are? How dare you challenge me? Your overconfidence has brought this fate upon you! Now you must face my wrath!'

As I got up on my bed, I tried to understand what was happening. Then, within the darkness, two glowing pieces of charcoal emerged at a distance. Yet, the pieces were not static. They seemed to float in the air, or rather, they seemed to dance! As a few moments passed, I understood that my pupils were dilating, and I was able to see through the obscure veil of darkness. I shuddered as I realized that the two simmering balls were actually a pair of vengeful eyes!

Then, in that nightly vision, I saw the ghastly figure of my mysterious assailant! The emaciated skeletal figure wore a long white robe, and stood close to me. Blood dripped from his gaping mouth as he growled ferociously, 'You think you are powerful? If so, then display your power! A power is powerful only when it is visible!'

I tried to stand up, but felt a numbness in my feet. I sat and stared at that gruesome apparition. I was unable to decipher what was occurring.

'You are a failure!' growled the ghoulish creature. 'Your life is a catastrophe! You have failed to do anything in life. Like a jumping monkey, you have been an unstable being. You are a disgrace, but you think your overconfidence is your shield. No, it is not so!'

A strange deadness overwhelmed my body. I gathered all my strength and tried to stand up. The devilish being held me and I felt a deathly coldness in his touch! Even his breath brushed against my skin with a stony frostiness.

'What is happening?' I deliberated. 'Who is he? Is this my final moment? Is this my encounter with death? What am I supposed to do?'

'Armageddon!' replied the creature. 'This is what you must do! There is no escape. I am your nemesis!'

'Who are you?' I shouted back with all my strength, and pushed back the ghastly apparition.

*It laughed an otherworldly laugh, and then said, **'I am… Jay Alani.'***

To my utter surprise, with the above-mentioned words, the

apparition became my own mirror image, like a magical swish. It laughed heartily once again, and yelled, 'My life has been a failure! I have failed everyone. I have miserably failed myself in everything I did. Now I have failed my Baba!'

Then, suddenly, the apparition evaporated into thin air but an echo of his voice lingered all around me... ***'Yet, my invisibility is my SUPERPOWER!'***

A blinding light blurred my vision and I sat up on my bed.

Truly, it was a bad dream. Perhaps the worst dream I have ever had. My head pained due to a hangover caused by drinking too much alcohol. I sat and sweated profusely while my heart palpitated hysterically.

Yes, it was my subconscious mind—my own GHOST—that had just haunted me! Despite trying to do so many things (some days a news anchor, on others, a writer; some days a reporter, on yet others, an actor), I was a complete failure!

The ordeal of the previous night that happened only a few hours ago was too prominent, and I realized the reason for the tormenting episode!

I hid my face within my palms and cried. However, my tears stopped an hour later. The new dawn of a new year was ahead. I wiped off the teardrops from my cheeks and repeated the line: ***'Yet, my invisibility is my SUPERPOWER!'***

I didn't understand what it truly meant inside my heart. However, destiny knew what it was supposed to mean to me and my life!

Maybe my life is the Armageddon, and myself, my arch-nemesis.

31 December 2014, 'Maurya Lok', Patna, Midnight

A Shocking Revelation

Revelry, revelry and never-ending revelry!

It was New Year's Eve. It was time to say goodbye to the year of 2014, and welcome in the new year. Hardly did I know that the year ahead was destined to mark the beginning of a nerve-wracking journey into the unknown.

I was suddenly feeling happy about the future. The previous year, precisely, the entirety of 2014, had been like a nightmare to me. I tried my hands at so many jobs, but miserably failed every time. In 2014, I tried to work in media, but failed. I tried to work as a content writer but failed. I tried to work as a voice artist but failed. Finally, when nothing was working out for me, my Baba called me back home from Delhi to work in his construction company. But once again, I failed, and this time, I failed him too!

I collected the whisky, the snacks, the cigarettes, the cake and the disposable plastic glasses, and stocked it up in a pile inside my car, and then arrived at the predetermined location to meet my best buddies. Yes, they were my childhood pals, namely Luv, Rahul and Anish. The four of us were a gang of rowdy youngsters who were always in the mood for some pure fun! Out of the four of us, Rahul was the ever-famished Godzilla who mercilessly gorged upon food. Hence, a lion's share of our booty was meant to end up inside his belly.

I picked up the guys and then we drove off to a secluded location near the highway. It was the perfect spot to engage in some revelry. With nobody to apprehend us, the booze could shower like a waterfall into our thirsty mouths, while our eyes could get a glimpse of the distant city lights and the occasional firework. As we gorged upon the food, I could feel a subtle sense of melancholy that gripped everything. In fact, an all-encompassing silence befell us, and none of us spoke. We just sat, ate and drank! We were in isolation, despite being together.

This prolonged silence was becoming intolerable, and I yelled, 'What is wrong with everyone? Why are you guys behaving like you have lost everything? Can anyone please say something?'

I had no idea, but a *Pandora's Box* was just flung open…

As we got out of the car, Anish looked into my eyes and said 'I don't know about the others, but I had an argument with my parents, and then the whole day, I was fighting with my girlfriend over the phone about our future. I know she has a good job and is earning well, but I am still a trainee. In the industry where I work, growth is really slow. So I am worried and am going through a tough time emotionally.'

'Oh, come on!' I said while the alcohol aggravated my adrenaline rush. 'Really? Is that all you are worried about? I mean, we are just about 25 years old and we will manage something decent in our careers! We all have the power to do something good in life.'

A grinding silence befell us, and I could see the eyes of my pals were becoming weirder. They were visibly trying to camouflage something. Yet, the moments of hide-and-seek were soon over. Rahul gulped down his drink and looked into my eyes.

'Look Jay, your life is easier than that of ours. You have a well-to-do father who also owns a business, and you are the only son he has!' said Rahul.

The words struck my chest and pierced through my heart. The shrapnel of his words continued to strike me, 'I mean, maybe you are not worried about your life as much as we are! See, we don't have a father who owns a business which can actually secure our futures, or maybe, at least give us a chance to experiment with different ventures! You know, even if you are not able to do something, you still have a good backup plan.'

My heart screamed, even though my mouth remained shut… '*No, I am not a man to piggyback on a rich father. I am not an irresponsible boy with fancy dreams! I am a man with a mission and I shall prove it one day!*'

'Perhaps Rahul is not being able to communicate properly. I know what he means. We are only saying that in this new year, we should focus more on our futures, rather than just wasting our time every single evening, doing nothing for hours.' Luv finally came up with a clear picture for me.

I didn't say a word in reply to Luv or to anyone else. I understood where the conversation was heading. I was the one who always invited the gang for our evening rendezvous. Hence, from their perspective, I was the spoilt brat who was also wasting their valuable time. I was the culprit who needed to be removed from their midst. Oh, what a shock! What shame!

With a shattered heart, I just went back to my car, ignited the engine and left without even saying goodbye to them. After driving for a few miles, I stopped near a culvert and wept like a child… Yes, I cried aloud in that secluded, dark night—New Year's eve! I rang up Priyanka, my sweetheart, who was a pillar of support, yet I was inconsolable. Even she failed to stop the bleeding in my heart. In my life, there were only two things that glued me together. First, it was Priyanka's undeterred love. Second, my unadulterated love for seeking the truth behind paranormal reality. That night, even Priyanka's love failed to soothe me. I was completely broken. The harsh daggers of reality had bruised my entire soul.

The year that was on its way out had made me a failure. It made me invisible! Nonetheless, I was oblivious to the fact that it was perhaps destined to be a boon for me. It was destined to be my **SUPERPOWER**.

1 January 2015, Patna, 9.30 a.m.

A Demonic Paradox

Anish's calls went unnoticed as I slept. As I woke up, I saw 10 missed calls from him. I called him back and Anish spoke in an anxious voice, 'Jay, there is somebody who needs your help!'

Despite whatever happened the previous night, Anish was one person who respected my inclination towards exploring paranormal reality. Even though I was still a novice, my knowledge and love for the supernatural realm was profound. Many ignorant folks considered me a follower of *aghor tantra*, or somebody who engaged in acts of black magic. I never paid much heed to such notions. I knew if destiny ever gave me an opportunity, I would do everything in my power to curb blind faith and bring out the truth behind paranormal reality.

Anish was aware of the developments in the field of paranormal investigations in the Western world. He respected my convictions and had always been confident about my capabilities in that domain. Perhaps that is the precise reason why he chose to call me that morning.

Anish sent me a number and asked me to call the person immediately. I could decipher the urgency in his voice and followed his words. I dialled the number and the call got connected…

'Hello…' A male voice responded from the other end.

'Hello, my name is Jay Alani. Actually, Anish has given me your number.'

'Yes, yes,' came the response.

'Please tell me, how can I help you?' I asked.

'Are you a tantric baba?' the person asked nervously.

'No, I am a paranormal investigator,' I answered. Yet I realized that he didn't quite understand what I meant.

After a few seconds of silence, I decided to explain it to him in more simple terms. 'Actually, I try to help people who are facing some kind of paranormal problem, hauntings, or other issues related to ghosts and the supernatural realm, approaching these in a more logical and scientific way.'

'Perhaps I don't fully understand everything,' arrived the reply. 'But that is insignificant. I desperately need help and you are like a messiah. My family and I are facing a far greater challenge. Fate has inflicted a horrific jolt upon us. We have tried everything but nothing seemed to work! Spells from the tantric baba and the sacrificial *yajna* have all failed miserably. We are at our wits' end…'

'Hold on,' I stopped him. 'Please tell me everything. I need to know the entire story.'

'My name is Ankit Bhatia,' he replied. 'I am a professional fitness coach at a local gym. I have three sisters. Our parents are no more, and we live with our grandmother. Life was progressing normally for us until catastrophe struck three days ago.'

Ankit paused for a moment and said, 'Pooja, my youngest sister, has become possessed by a horrific paranormal entity! Three days ago, she went to attend a friend's birthday party. That night, after dinner, she returned home and went to sleep. However, from the next morning, a series of unexplainable episodes began to take place.'

I listened to Ankit with the utmost patience while he continued. 'She started to scream in a horrendous male voice while her body shook with convulsions! She bruised and scratched her entire body with her own nails and teeth. Her otherworldly howls were like the wails of the devil. Oh... it is terrible!'

I could clearly understand the apprehension in Ankit's voice. He seemed to be choking as he spoke. 'This sight is unbearable to us. For the last few days, we have lost our sleep and our appetite. Everyone in the family is overpowered with grief. Shockingly, the ghost inside her has made her a monster. She is gorging on food and water, and is behaving like an animal. Our neighbours are scared to even speak with us. We have been ostracized, and are living a reclusive life of extreme distress. Jay, I fear that my poor sister Pooja is dying—she needs help or else she will perish!'

I knew that the onslaught of a paranormal possession happened in stages. However, it is always an extreme level of haunting. There was something that was bothering my subconscious mind, but I was unable to understand it. Yet I chose to dive into the case.

Ankit wept like a child and said, 'Despite our inadequate income, we have spent thousands of rupees in these two days.

Alas, everything has failed. My little Pooja continues to moan like a creature from hell while she screams out a name—Ashish.'

In that instant, I stopped Ankit and asked sharply, 'Who is Ashish?'

A perplexed Ankit responded, 'I don't know. No one in our family has ever know anybody named Ashish. Yet, with red bulging eyes, she howls his name and then her demonic laughter reverberates across the entire house! It is so gruesome. Shivers of fear ripple through my body as I relate it to you.'

'That is most intriguing!' I replied. 'Now listen to me carefully. Within a few hours, I shall visit you. However, nobody must know about it. Moreover, you must lock up Pooja inside her room. She must go without any food or water until I arrive.'

A scared Ankit asked, 'Are you sure that she won't harm herself? I am really afraid.'

I comforted him and said confidently, 'Be fearless. Pooja will be all right. The ghost will abandon her forever. Trust me!'

The reassurance in my voice calmed Ankit while my own soul prepared me for a weird challenge. Only my heart knew that I was about to engage in a bizarre 'gamble'!

Two Hours Later

An Encounter with the 'Demon'

Ankit's location was about 20 kilometres from my house. Within the next two hours, I quickly freshened up, got dressed and rushed out. My intuition told me that I would be able to solve the case. With an overdose of confidence, I amplified the volume of the music and drove down to my destination.

Ankit met me outside the gates of their house. The locality was somewhat shabby, courtesy of the adjacent slums, and Ankit's house was also in a state of utter disrepair owing to the sheer lack of maintenance. It reflected their financial struggles. We entered the house and I noticed the decrepit condition of the interiors. A few women of various ages sat in the living room. Perhaps they were expecting the arrival of a tantric baba. So my appearance visibly disheartened them.

I sat down on a chair and looked at everyone for a while. Then I turned towards Ankit and asked, 'Has there been any other incidence of paranormal possession in your family?'

One of the women returned a surprised look, and replied, 'Yes…but how do you know?'

'Time is running out,' I said sternly. 'So if you want to save Pooja, then please cooperate and answer my questions.'

There was shock in everyone's eyes. The woman stammered, 'It was…Ranjana. She was possessed by a ghost once. However, she got better within a day, after we took her to a tantric!'

Ankit added nervously, 'Yes, Ranjana is my elder sister.'

'I am Ranjana.' A woman in her thirties interrupted Ankit and came forward.

I looked into her eyes for a while and then said in a dull voice, 'The demon seems to have established a deliberate connection with this family.'

Ranjana replied while tears rolled down from her eyes, 'I was returning alone from my in-laws' house. It was almost evening, and the twilight was receding fast into the darkness. Then…the wind caught me! *Hawa lag gayi*… I couldn't understand what happened, but everyone knows that I became a victim of a painful paranormal possession!'

The conversations went on for some more time, and then I asked Ankit, 'Where is Pooja?'

Ankit pointed towards a locked door and said, 'She is inside that room. As per your instructions, we have kept her locked inside.'

'Quick, give me some holy vermillion and a glass of Gangajal,' I said. 'We must not waste any more time.'

Ranjana and another woman quickly brought me the things. I took out a piece of sacred cloth, and tied it across my neck. I covered my forehead with some vermilion and took the glass of Gangajal with me. Only I knew what I was doing. Then, as Ankit opened the door, my heart started beating faster and I entered the room. Next, I turned back momentarily and said, 'Now wait for me here…and lock the door from outside!'

Ankit obeyed my words while everyone else stood anxiously outside.

As I went in and approached the bed, I saw Pooja. She was asleep. I noticed the bruises on her own body and her beautiful, untied hair. I silently looked around the entire room and then stood still.

Then, with a sudden impulse, I splashed some of the holy water on Pooja's face! The jolt was abrupt and Pooja sat up on the bed. Then she madly shook her head while her hair whipped against my face.

She howled in an appalling male voice, and screamed, 'Go away! Leave me alone! Else I will kill this girl! If you try to do anything, I will bite and tear her body into pieces!'

Her eyes were red and fierce. He entire body trembled while the apparition tormented her like a tornado from within.

'What is in your hand?' she wailed angrily. 'Those are all useless! Go away!'

I stood still for the next five minutes while Ankit and the others waited outside and shivered with fear. I could even hear their cries.

Finally, I gathered all my strength, moved ahead and sat down on the bed with a thump. I sat close to Pooja, held her swiftly and whispered something into her ears. Then I released her from my grip, sat straight and laughed. 'Hahaha!'

My laughter reverberated across the room while Pooja cried out loudly. The deadly combination—her fierce wails and my unhinged laughter—was just too ghastly. Finally, there was complete silence.

After 10 more minutes, I opened the door and came out. Everyone was looking bewildered. I waited a moment and then moved aside with a smile. Behind me stood Pooja, and she was perfectly all right!

I announced with confidence, 'Pooja is completely healed. The demonic possession is over!'

Everyone rushed towards her and hugged her. Tears rolled down Ankit's cheeks and he hugged me like a child. With an ecstatic feeling, he blurted out, 'How did you do this? What had happened to her? Will the devil ever return? How much should I pay you? Jay, I am so relieved! Thank you so much! You are truly a messiah.'

I shook hands with him and replied calmly, 'The ordeal is over, forever! Trust me, no demon will ever return. Pooja will vouch for that. And, she will tell you everything. Moreover, I don't charge for my investigations. I am happy that I could help you and your family.'

Saying these words, I walked out. A melancholy mood possessed me and I got into the car to come home.

Earlier That Day, Patna

The Conspiracy

Honestly, Pooja was never a victim of paranormal possession. She was a collaborator in an act that is called 'paranormal conspiracy'. In simpler terms, she was faking it. The entire episode was a deliberate drama that the young 16-year-old girl had enacted brilliantly. Yet the question remained—why?

As I sat on my bed that night and reflected on everything that happened during the day, my mind flew back to my conversation with Pooja's family just before I entered her room.

Flashback

'Then…the wind caught me! I couldn't understand what happened, but everyone knows that I became the victim of a painful paranormal possession!' Ranjana had said.

Before I could ask further, a young girl (I presumed that she was Ankit's second sister) added with excitement, 'Yes, that day Ranjana-Didi had a big fight with her family and was leaving their house forever!'

Ranjana shot a glare at the girl but I interrupted her and asked, 'So let me get this straight, you had a fight with your in-laws and your husband, you left their house and you came here. While you were coming back, you got possessed by the demonic spirit. Is that exactly what happened?'

A visibly irritated Ranjana replied sternly, 'That is irrelevant to this situation! Please focus on the problem at hand and deal with what has befallen Pooja.'

I ignored her words and asked firmly, 'So after you got better, why didn't you return once the scuffle was over?'

'My husband was a drunkard and used to torture me,' shrieked Ranjana. 'It was like living in hell. So I never went back. The torment was harrowing. I got divorced thereafter.'

Ankit joined the conversation and added, 'Our family tantric told us that the demonic spirit in possession of Ranjana would consume her body and soul if she ever returned and faced the torture again! We were very scared. So...'

I raised my hand and terminated the conversation. I had found the answer that I was seeking.

Right from the moment when Ankit mentioned an unknown person named Ashish, I suspected that Pooja's case was one of paranormal conspiracy. While speaking with Ankit, I dug up and scanned through Pooja's social media handles. Despite the lack of any suspicious activity, I noticed an elusive male presence in her photos and posts. I presumed the context and went ahead with my 'gamble'.

That Day, inside Pooja's Room

My laughter reverberated across the house while Pooja cried out loudly. The deadly combination of the horrible harmony was too ghastly. Finally, there was complete silence...

I looked at her and said in a confident yet ruthless voice, 'Pooja, I know everything about Ashish. I also know you are faking all this and I have your pictures with him on Facebook. For your information, I met Ashish before coming here and he has told me everything. Right now, he is in police custody!'

It was a lie. So I paused a bit and then added animatedly, 'Now either tell me the truth, or else the police will walk in with Ashish and arrest both of you! They will expose everything to your brother and to your family. Hence, your only option is to tell me the truth!'

This subtle act on my part worked wonders. She revealed everything. I learnt that Ranjana had an affair with the family tantric. However, she was married to a man who indeed used to torture her. When she ultimately left her in-laws' house, they conspired together to fake the paranormal possession.

Then a 16-year-old Pooja fell in love with a boy named Ashish. The latter belonged to a lower caste and was also a mere peon. His social and financial status was too weak, and Pooja knew that her family would never accept their relationship. Thus she teamed up with Ranjana and her lover the tantric. Pooja knew about their affair and became a confidante. Hence, Ranjana helped her devise the entire plan so that she could get married to Ashish.

I listened to everything and told her calmly, 'Pooja, you are a little girl. You are not the age to get married. This fake drama has already cost your family ₹20,000! Despite that, think about the mental torment this has subjected them to. Listen to me carefully—I will go out with you and tell everyone that you are all right. But you must admit everything yourself. They are your family. They will accept your wishes. Speak with Ankit separately. Your brother loves you a lot. Now promise me.'

Pooja made a promise to me and kept it too. A few days later, Ankit called me up and told me everything. I felt happy. He told me, 'Like an invisible superhero, you have solved the biggest problem in our lives!'

Paranormal conspiracies were, and still are, a big threat to society. Paranormal possessions never happen the way popular perception dictates. Only the eradication of blind faith can dispel such myths.

January, 2015, Patna, A Week Later

The New Dawn

As I sat inside my room, I looked into the mirror. My eyes searched for my own GHOST. Yet the ghost was invisible. Perhaps it was inside me.

After the superlative success of my investigation, my heart convinced my mind, '*Jay, you were born to be different. You were born to be a PARANORMAL INVESTIGATOR! You were born to fight and remove blind faith! Like an invisible superhero, you must strive to fulfil this passionate dream.*'

Every GHOST was once a HUMAN.

Yet, in the realm of the unknown, their obscure forms render them paranormal in nature.

I knew I could understand their elusive existence in a manner that was mutually respectful.

Yes, it was my invisible SUPERPOWER!

2

Hell's Gate

The 'Path to Heaven' goes past the 'Gateway to Hell'.

May 2015

The Legend Surfaces

Located near the Vasai Creek, Vasai Fort was about eight kilometres from Naigaon East Station. Off the main route of Killa Road, it stood like a solitary vampire, savouring the residues of a bygone era. The large tree—with its dry branches spread out like the hands of an emaciated corpse—stood to welcome in any visitors. The fort had so many secrets hidden in its womb. Behind the fort was a dense forest. Girdling the forest were a few small villages.

As I stood outside and stared at the magnificent Vasai Fort with awestruck eyes, an old beggar woman came and stood beside me. Astonishingly, she had no intention of asking for money. I was startled by her sudden arrival. She looked at me for a few moments and then spoke in an animated voice.

'Many years ago, a woman lived in one of those villages. She had great powers that were misunderstood by the foolish men of that era. She could tame the deadliest of snakes by just

quivering her fingers. She could charm them with her persona. She shared a bond of love with the wild serpents. In return, they obeyed her orders. It was a strength that made her powerful, and she silently became a weapon for the ruthless society of the time. It was said that in exchange for money, she fulfilled the dark desires of many men and women. She exercised her powers and unleashed her serpents on their rivals. Her weird chants could be heard from within the dull darkness of her hut. It sounded echoes of dread within the hearts of the villagers. But she got marked as a witch and came to be shunned by society!'

She stopped for a moment and then continued with a fervent energy, 'She went mad in her greed for power, but her divine powers became her biggest foe. She was labelled as a chudail by the terrified villagers, and was openly scorned! Legend has it that the serpent-shaped metal ring that she wore on her left index finger was the insignia of her witchcraft. She left an impression of that insignia wherever she struck. Then one fateful day, the hysterical villagers decided to hunt down the chudail and punish her. Their wrath was great, and the poor soul felt helpless. Perhaps she was not harmless, but the law of the kingdom never had enough proof to convict her. More certainly, villagers were not empowered by God to punish her! Alas, the misfortune befell her and she knew that her doom was near!'

With a sudden act of reflex, the woman clutched my right arm and said, 'The fury in the eyes of her attackers was ruthless, and she was powerless before them. She ran madly across the forest, entered Vasai Fort and reached the centre of the vast structure. Here, a huge well sat with its gaping mouth. As she heard her attackers enter the fort, she perhaps chose not to be slaughtered at the hands of those mortal demons. She jumped into the well and ended her own life! Two or three days later, her decomposed body was recovered by the police. Thereafter, it has been said that her frantic soul started to haunt the fort. In the eerie atmosphere of the fort, many visitors have noticed her apparition at night. The ghastly spirit bellowed at them in anger.'

My vision grew hazy as I listened to the story. It was a sad and shattering tale. I wanted to know more, so moments later, I turned towards her to ask her a few questions. But then my heart leapt in disbelief as I saw that she was gone—the old beggar woman seemed to have evaporated! The abruptness of her disappearance shook me to the core.

As I stood there, stunned by a shock that froze me, I told myself, 'I must find out an answer.'

Three Months Ago

The Journey

The cage of my mind rattled like a bird-box!

With an overwhelming mix of aspirations and apprehensions, I started my journey towards Mumbai—the city of dreams! My conscious mind constantly deliberated with my subconscious mind, while my heart reflected on the future that I was heading towards.

I sat by the open window of the train's compartment. As the gigantic locomotive made its way out of the station, the dark, opaque shroud of night covered the landscape that it passed. Only the clattering din of the metallic wheels screamed loudly—like the howls of a monstrous ghost.

The uncertainties wreaking havoc in my mind joined that

cacophony and tried hard to discourage me from taking this drastic step that I was in the process of taking. As the train continued to gain speed, images of past incidents and face-offs whizzed past my eyes like the high-speed images taken by a fast-motion camera. They flung me into a state of trance.

Yet my ever-present self-confidence and uncanny courage told me, '*Jay, you have taken this decision. Whatever comes ahead will be the outcome of your own choice. Nobody needs to be praised or blamed for it. Go ahead and fulfil your motto.*'

Then, the disparate images appeared in a flashback as memories flooded my mind.

The eve of 31 December 2014 witnessed a thunderbolt from the sky that shattered the glass walls of my fragile world. That night, I understood that our lives are solitary journeys.

My fried Rahul's words pierced my heart: 'Look, Jay, your life is easier than those of ours. You have a well-to-do father who also owns a business, and you are the only son he has!'

The shrapnel of his words struck me hard, 'I mean, maybe you are not worried about your life as much as we are! See, we don't have a father who owns a business which can actually secure our futures, or maybe at least give us a chance to experiment with different ventures! You know, even if you are not able to do something, you still have a good backup plan.'

My heart screamed that night, even though my mouth remained shut. '*No, I am not a man to piggyback on a rich father. I am not an irresponsible boy with fancy dreams! I am a man with a mission and I shall prove it one day!*'

Two months later, a fortnight before I left home…

I was in the living room. I looked into my father's eyes and said, 'Baba, I have made my decision. I am taking up paranormal investigation as my profession. It is a passion that

I want to explore. To do so, I must go to Mumbai.'

As I sat on the sofa with a visibly distraught face, Baba said in his grim voice, 'Jay, I understand that you have already made up your mind. Nevertheless, you need to take responsibility for your own fate. There is always a place for you in my business. However, I will not invest the family's hard-earned money in this uncertain and untested, yet expensive, aspiration of yours. I will not stop you from doing what you wish to do. However, you need to seek out your own path on your own.'

I nodded like an obedient boy who had taken a drastic decision. Again, I didn't say anything.

The memories were harsh but they hardened my resolve. As I slipped away into the realms of sleep, everything vanished in a thin mist.

I knew that survival was going to be tough in Mumbai. However, my self-confidence told me, '*Jay, you are very talented. Go and make a difference!*' With this superlative conviction, I sat down to forge a plan for my future. My objective was to establish paranormal reality as a successful subset within the creative industry. I was certain that creating a paranormal investigation programme was possible. I wanted to make my own television show, and I was very sure that I would succeed. It was not the greed for fame that drove me. I didn't choose to go to Mumbai to become a celebrity. I wanted to use the powers of the creative industry in Mumbai to reach out to an audience in such a way that my voice would be able to eliminate blind faith and establish the truths of paranormal reality.

I was inexperienced with respect to the many truths that were awaiting me. Maybe destiny planned to test my mettle through a journey that I had never imagined. I only knew that

I must make myself into a *brand*! Yes, a brand that would be associated with honesty and truth.

Some questions kept troubling me. Why would people listen to me? How would I make this career financially viable? I wanted to take it up as a career, but didn't want to charge my clients for carrying out paranormal investigations. That was as good as being a modern-day tantric baba! No, I didn't want to become one of them.

I told myself, '*I shall never charge people any money. I shall use the content of my work and showcase it through various creative channels. It would fetch me credibility and financial stability. That is why Mumbai is the best place to start my mission.*'

With the possibility of any financial support eliminated by Baba, I had another difficult hurdle to overcome. I was in dire need of funds. I was pretty sure that within a few months, I would be able to convince a potential production house to back me, and my career would take off. Thus, for the initial three or four months, I needed to watch my expenses.

My soulmate Priyanka—the one person who had been beside me through thick and thin—was the first to extend her unending support to me. She even gave me ₹15,000. I was in a frenzy to prove myself, so I spoke with several friends and collected some funds from a few of them. Finally, I spoke with another person who had always been a source of support in my life—my brother-in-law. He lent me ₹10,000. I felt overjoyed. Tears rolled down my cheeks when I looked at the money I had gathered. To prove myself, I had literally begged for assistance despite belonging to a very respectable family.

Mumbai was completely alien to me. The first thing that

came to my mind was, '*Where will I find shelter in the huge cosmopolitan maze?*'

The only thing I'd found through my internet searches was that most of the production houses were in Andheri, Juhu or Bandra. However, finding accommodation in those posh locales would be financial suicide for me. I didn't want to stay as a paying guest. So I searched for a rented apartment. After a long search, I found something satisfactory. It was in a place called Naigaon. It was a 1-BHK apartment. The rent was ₹4,000, and the agent wanted a deposit of ₹10,000. My heart leapt with cheer when I found the flat and I instantly chose it. I paid the deposit and booked my tickets.

May 2015, Vasai Fort, 6.00 p.m.

As the Exploration Began...

Adrenaline gushed through my body. As it reached its peak...

A week ago, I got my first clue about the hauntings at Vasai Fort. That moment was ethereal and I decided to plunge myself into exploring the truth. Yet this time, I needed proper instruments to do my work. I didn't want to be an amateur. This was my opportunity to become a professional. I checked my funds and ordered an EMF meter and a digital thermometer through an online portal. With a heart full of excitement, I studied online videos to learn how to use them.

The next five days acted as a preparatory period. For the first time, I was going to use such professional gadgets. I needed to be fully prepared before taking the plunge.

Within my heart, there was always an absence of fear with respect to the world of the paranormal. Perhaps the world where spirits existed was as independent as the one where we lived. My mission was to eliminate blind faith and shed light upon the truth. With this mission in mind, I had decided the date and time of my operation at Vasai Fort. Then the old beggar woman's vanishing act further intensified my curiosity.

I entered the premises of the fort around 6.00 p.m.

As I looked around, I honestly felt that the atmosphere was certainly not a welcoming one. The entire location was peopled with shady couples and rowdy local youths. I didn't feel like looking at them as it made me feel uncomfortable. I focused on my work and surveyed the entire place. Vasai Court was nearby, and I figured out that if I used my flashlight indiscriminately during my investigation at night, I was sure to attract the ire of the patrolling policemen there. I made a brief plan in my mind and went out. I knew I must return a few hours later, when all the unwanted human presence would be gone from the premises.

At 9.00 p.m. sharp, I re-entered the fort. This time, it was completely deserted. Under the veil of darkness, everything looked dreadfully serene. The ruins of the fort appeared like lifeless carcasses whose eternal peace was being disturbed by my sudden appearance. I explored the whole place once again in that completely different atmosphere. In the absence of light, even a harmless piece of rock looked like a phantom. A bizarre panorama was unfolding in that colossal arena.

I walked past the public area, crossed the citadel and reached a large space that was probably an open hall. A few graves were scattered around it. Time had worn off their identities, but the tombstones proclaimed their presence. I crossed the surrounding shrubbery and switched on my digital thermometer and EMF meter. It recorded a slight temperature drop, but I knew that it was normal in any secluded place.

Then, all of a sudden, the EMF meter started to flash! One by one, all the lights started to blink! My heart beat faster and I turned the device towards every corner of the fort. Honestly, in that completely remote place, I felt a shiver running down my spine. It was my first time using the device. A few minutes passed and then, all of a sudden, I sensed a presence behind myself!

I turned around quickly and saw three men standing behind me. From the odour of their breaths and their wobbly gait, it was clear to me that they were very drunk. They spoke in Marathi among themselves and looked at me suspiciously.

As they questioned me, I revealed my honest intentions. I told them that I was new in Mumbai and was an aspiring paranormal investigator. To gain their confidence, I said, 'I am here to do a solo investigation and I hope this will get me good footage.'

The men could relate to my attitude and continued the conversation for about half an hour. Finally, one of the guys said, 'The witch really is a personification of horror! A few months ago, my friend Arjun saw her with his own eyes! She was a fearful figure in a white saree, and had a mutilated face that spewed the wrath of revenge! The shock was massive and he fainted. Fortunately, we knew where he had gone. When he didn't return, we started to look for him. We found him here, in front of the well, and took him home. For the next three days, he had a high fever and was sick for weeks!'

At last, after a bit more of their gibberish, they left and I was relieved to have been left alone. I sighed in relief. I needed this privacy to carry out my investigation. I looked at my watch again. It was almost 11.00.

3 Months Ago

The Arrival

Thus I reached Mumbai—the city of dreams! I set foot at the railway station in this majestic city with a heart full of ideas, awe and unbound happiness.

I had lived in Delhi, the capital of our country. Yet this place stunned me with its uniqueness as soon as I reached! Walking out of Mumbai Central Station, I stood still and caught a glimpse of its enthralling surroundings. For a moment, I felt an alarming chill—*could I indeed realize my dream here?*

There were a few thousand bucks in my pocket. With no acquaintances and no concrete plan in mind, I took my suitcase and started walking.

As I stepped out, I hired a taxi. I got in, mentioned the address of my destination in Naigaon East and asked, 'What is the fare?'

The driver replied nonchalantly, '₹2,000.'

My heart leapt within my ribcage and I asked involuntarily, 'What? Why so much? Is it that far away?'

'Sir, it is more than 50 kilometres from here, and takes almost two hours to reach!' exclaimed the driver.

Despite being close enough to the railway station, the distance to my new residence in Naigaon East shocked me. Living here meant that I would need to commute a long way to Mumbai proper where all the studios were located.

The broker Ramu, who had arranged my accommodation, was a nice person. He took me to the 11th floor of a residential building and opened a door. The building was not very old and was sparsely occupied. I was amazed to see the apartment that I had landed. It was a miniscule piece of real estate that I would occupy for ₹4,000 a month. With a super-small balcony, and just a single room furnished with a single electric fan and a single tube-light, this place could well be compared to a birdcage.

From Ramu, I understood that the local trains of Mumbai were my best option to carry out my daily commute.

'Get yourself a second-class pass for the local trains. The station can be reached on foot, or you can take an auto-rickshaw. You only need to cross the ditch and you will reach Naigaon East Station within seven minutes,' concluded Ramu with a wide grin.

Now that the first problem was solved, I had to seek the answer to the bigger problem. I needed work—work that would establish my career as a paranormal investigator. It was uncharted territory in India, and I had dared enter it without permission. The tricky questions and the doubtful looks were inevitable. *Paranormal...what? Is that supposed to be a field of work? Do people even trust these things? How do you make money from it?*

May 2015, Vasai Fort, 2.00 a.m.

'EEEEEeeeeeee!'

The shriek, followed by a 'Hissssss!', chilled me to the bone. In that split second, I felt a numbness shooting through my nerves. However, in another moment, I regained my command over them. It was the cry of some nocturnal bird, or an elusive serpent, mixed into an unnerving cacophony of unknown noises.

The buzzing insect world and the faint sounds of distant human voices were the only indication that a mortal world existed beyond the deathly hollowness of the deserted land where I was roaming.

The darkness engulfed everything around me while the silvery shroud of the moonlight sparkled upon the ruins of the fort. The citadel of Vasai Fort stood like a humongous monster in front of me. I was standing beside the infamous well where the doomed woman, who was labelled a witch, had sacrificed herself to escape from the clutches of the lunatic mob! That is history, but the periodic re-appearance of her spirit has become a myth. She was the chudail who haunted the place for revenge!

The old graveyard with its array of neglected graves was shining in the same moonlight. The remnants of the gravestones resembled the gaping mouths of their lingering spirits.

The EMF meter in my hand was flashing and blinking madly, but I didn't feel scared. I felt concerned. If this internationally acclaimed device had to be trusted, then I was indeed in the vicinity of a massive paranormal presence! At 2.00 a.m., my eyes scavenged for a glimpse of the truth.

The stench from the well was horrid. I felt sick to stand there and absorb that hellish odour. One minute passed... Two minutes passed... And then it happened! Yes, it did!

I felt a presence. It was certainly not my imagination. The feeling was as real as what one feels when somebody arrives while one is completely alone inside a huge, dark room! The façade of the adjoining chapel creaked. Perhaps some nocturnal animal was carelessly crossing it.

With a sudden flash of intuition, I ran... Without wasting any time, I ran in the direction in which I could sense the presence. With nothing in sight, I stopped momentarily and took a deep breath.

Then, like a gust of wind, or a flash of lightning, it whizzed past me. The rapid, invisible force pushed through the damp air, brushed over me and raised every hair on my body!

Yes, I felt someone cross my field of vision like a stray gust of wind. When I looked sideways, specifically to my right, I sensed that a pale figure (or maybe a white nothing) was revealing its existence to me! The shadow of that entity swept over my body. And, very close by, I clearly heard the sound of passing footsteps…

It was a shock! A shock that froze me—like a bone-chilling sigh brushing against my chest!

I turned to the right, the direction in which the movement took place. Even though I had not seen it clearly, I was sure that it was not a hoax. What I felt seemed to have a weird reality whose definition was unknown to me.

In such an eerie atmosphere, in the absence of humans, and in the dead of the night, the mind can play many tricks on the heart and mind. However, I grew very inquisitive. Honestly, I felt another spate of cold shivers run down my spine as I switched off my EMF meter and turned it back on. My eyes were not able to see anything unusual. However, once again, the EMF meter was flashing wildly.

In my heart of hearts, I had faith in the equipment I was carrying. A sudden drop in temperature recorded by the digital thermometer, the beeps of the EMF meter and an uncanny sensation all came together to tell me that I was very close to discovering my target. I could sense the presence of something substantial even through the pores of my skin. It seemed as if the sleeping souls inside those abandoned graves were all silently screaming in chorus, and saying something to me.

It was precisely 2.30 a.m. I convinced myself and turned around to take another round within the fort. My focus was specifically on the citadel beside the well. I steeled myself and switched off my flashlight because I needed discreet isolation for one last act of desperation.

Then, in that abysmal darkness, I started to stride ahead.

Two Months Ago

The rollercoaster ride lasted from February to April. The hour-long commutes to Andheri on local trains, followed by visits to production houses—it was a gruelling routine. Initially, I didn't get a response. However, I kept clinging to my hopes. The first production house to respond and actually listen to my project plan was located in Lokhandwala. I met the producer and delivered a fantastic presentation. The person asked me to email them the plan and I did so with high hopes. However, nothing happened thereafter. Thus began a saga of failed attempts—meeting after meeting, primarily with production houses, without much yield. I wanted an unbiased show with a touch of entertainment. However, the producers wanted showbiz. I even budged under the pressure and began to modify my plans. From the low response rate and a bit of my own experience up to that point, I understood that the decision-making power lay in the hands of the TV channels which commissioned the shows. So I started to directly reach out to them, but I never got a better result.

With depleting funds, I was frustrated and miserable. At times, I asked for money from friends. However, it was becoming a desperate effort for survival. Baba helped me a few times; he had always loved me unconditionally. Yet I was scared to ask him for more, fearing that he would tell me to return! I was completely exhausted financially and emotionally. I was almost at my wits' end.

One night, as I alighted at Naigaon Station and started to walk, I saw a man selling tiffin and tea. I stood at his stall and spoke to him. To my surprise, I discovered that he was a struggling actor who had chosen to set up this food-cart business to support himself financially. It earned him about ₹500 to ₹700 daily. I thanked him for sharing this idea with me. In my desperation, I liked it. It needed an investment of around ₹3,000 to ₹4,000. The next day was a Saturday, and I had some time in my hands. So I borrowed some money from a friend. And with an anxious mind, I grew determined and got a cart of my own over the weekend.

Hence, from the following Monday, I stared my own food-cart in the hopes of making some money to aid my survival. Under this new regime, I left Andheri every evening around 5.00 p.m., reached Naigaon, and sat with my food-cart from 7.00 p.m. till midnight. I positioned my cart across the road from Naigaon East Station. My business was simple. I only sold tea and eggs. Surprisingly, on the first day, I earned

₹300. I wept like a child on seeing the money that I needed so desperately.

Such was my despondency that I began to skip lunch. Only two proper meals a day led my body to collapse, but it was all I could afford. Between hawking at the gates of potential producers, sending around 500 presentations, and running my own business, I was getting trampled on by life.

End of April, 2015

I was exhausted. After two months in Mumbai, I knew that I was completely broken. With no work and no money, I was bankrupt. With a sunken soul and a mind full of fears, I wept like a child. That morning, I had visited a person at a popular studio, but when I came out of the meeting, I realized that I didn't have a single penny in my pocket. As I sat on the footpath and cried, the man walked up to me and clasped my shoulders. He offered me lunch and even lent me some money. It was a moment when I truly felt as if… I was a beggar.

The gateway to hell was indeed in front of me.

Fate does have a plan for everyone. Hence, the following day, I came across some bizarre news as I sat beside my cart.

It was around 7.30 p.m.; three men arrived at my cart and ordered some eggs and tea. From their conversation and accent, I figured out that they were locals and were speaking in Marathi. As I prepared their food, I overheard their conversation. From fragments of English and Hindi words like 'haunted', 'fort' and 'ghost', I derived something that ignited a spark in my heart. I served them the food and directly asked them about the subject of their discussion.

Thus unfolded a tale that was to become an integral part of my own journey! The story was of a fabled witch or chudail who supposedly haunted Vasai Fort. Such was the terror that she inspired that many feared to visit the place even during the day. The story was intriguing and I went home with dreams in my eyes.

My subconscious mind fervently said to me, 'Jay, this is an opportunity that you must explore! A paranormal investigation, right here in Mumbai, would be the perfect example of your work and your mission! Go ahead!'

My conscious mind cried out, 'Jay, don't hurry! Great wars need great weapons. Only then can victory become certain. For a proper paranormal investigation, you need professional tools.'

May 2015, Vasai Fort, 3.15 a.m.

Final Exploit

I entered the citadel. The darkness seemed much denser in its interior. My devices were actively screaming at me. To get a proper understanding of the entity I was looking for, I switched them off. In that moment, the unblemished darkness was accompanied by an abysmal silence. Beads of sweat appeared on my forehead.

Then, a few more minutes later came the zenith of my investigation.

Outside the wall, amidst the bushes that were very close me, I heard the heavy sound of someone running. It was too prominent a sound to be ignored, and it seemed to belong to something running on two legs. In a moment, I switched on my

EMF meter and saw that all the lights were flashing. That was it. The situation demanded an immediate response.

Without wasting a second, I ran out. Alas, my eyes failed to catch a glimpse of anything. But a gust of icy wind whizzed past me, as if a tempest was rushing out of the area. Was it just the wind, or was it the sigh of an apparition? Perhaps I will never know!

Nonetheless, it was very much real. I switched off the EMF meter once again.

I stood there and panted, trying to catch my breath. But before I could perceive anything else, I felt a sharp pain in my upper back. It was a painful prick. I was clueless about what had just happened.

The next moment, something fell near my feet and I quickly switched on my flashlight. To my sheer horror, I saw that it was a big snake. With utter fear, I realized that I was bitten by it. I touched my wound and saw that blood was oozing out of it. A sensation of fear gripped me. The snake was perhaps on the outer wall of the fort, and fell on me when I rushed out.

However, even in that horrific moment, my eyes fell upon the dilapidated wall. Within the illuminated halo cast by my flashlight, I clearly saw a shadow... Yes, it was the definite outline of a woman on the wall. That shadow asserted its existence in my conscious and subconscious mind, and I fell down on the ground. It perhaps remained in front of my eyes for an entire minute, and then faded away.

As I grasped my instruments and sat there, I started to cry. Other intriguing questions started popping up in my mind. Now what? What will I tell others? Where will the money for my treatment come from?

Yet, I must acknowledge that even in that instant of utter misery, I felt an ecstasy—my first paranormal investigation in Mumbai was not a failure.

Despite the unfortunate snake-bite, I was euphoric that I HAD DONE A GOOD JOB. The shadow of the woman, the presence of the snake on the wall, and then the snake-bite that seemed to be a manifestation of her vengeance—together, they were proof enough that I had succeeded in my mission.

As I dragged myself out into the main road outside Vasai Fort, in the faint aura of the streetlights, I saw a local temple. I limped past it towards Vasai Court. A biker riding down Killa Road saw me and took me to the local hospital. The doctor at the Emergency Department removed the snake's tooth from the wound, and gave me some initial medication. He listened to my description of the serpent and told me that it was perhaps non-venomous.

Then, as I was preparing to leave, the doctor softly held my shoulders, came close to me and said in a grim voice, 'It is so strange… I have never seen an injury like this. It looks as if the wound is surrounded by a deep impression of a ring!'

I couldn't reply to him, so I left. As I came out and reached the railway station, I could finally comprehend the depth of his words and laughed heartily. *The path to heaven indeed goes past the gateway to hell.*

3

Warrior or Surivor

He who is a 'survivor' conquers himself to be the mightiest 'warrior'.

9 December 2016, Ahmedabad, 9.45 p.m.

The Confrontation

Anukriti, the young 23-year-old girl, had returned from college a few hours ago and had finished her quiet dinner with her mother. Then she went inside her own bedroom and stretched herself on her bed. Winters in Ahmedabad are never too intense, but the winds were slightly chilly in the early weeks of December. Anukriti pulled the sheet up over her body, switched off the light, and kept the table-lamp on. She picked up a book and tried to read a little.

After a tiring day, she felt a bit exhausted but was not sleepy. She decided to read a little so that her mind could relax and she could go to sleep. However, as she skimmed through the pages, her brain felt sceptical and her heart began to beat wildly. It was the same uncanny feeling that she was experiencing in an intense way for the past few days.

In the dim light of the low-powered electric lamp, the shadows of the furniture seemed like monstrous creatures standing across the room. Anukriti tried to eliminate all the negative thoughts and forced her mind to focus on the book. Outside, it was dark. Most of the households in the neighbourhood had already slipped into the world of sleep. The silence in the air was gripping, and a few hoots from nocturnal birds added to the atmosphere of spookiness. Perhaps her mother was also asleep in the adjacent room. And then, something happened...

Anukriti saw it in front of her eyes. It was the outline of a man. Yes, she was sure of it! A huge human figure was standing in front of her. At first, it appeared to be a dark shadow, but then it slowly metamorphosed into a human form. With a distorted face twisting into a strange, ghastly grin displaying an array of teeth, the figure grew more and more conspicuous. Anukriti knew the man very well. She had loved him her entire life. Yes, he was her hero...

In a moment of horror, the book fell from her hands and she uttered a quiet cry, 'Baba, is it really you?' The figure didn't reply. It stared at her with stone-cold eyes and stood motionless. But something else was unfolding behind it. It was the outline of something else, or rather, somebody else. The shadow of this individual was gigantic. It was monstrous. It was as if the devil was standing behind him. As a reddish glow filled the room, the figure of the huge creature began to assume a shape. It had a ghastly face with protruding teeth, and skin that was red like smouldering charcoal. For a moment, it became visible and seemed to resemble a hybrid between a human and a serpent. With a horrific face, it pointed its serpent-like fingers at Anukriti and breathed fire. Then it vanished. Yes, it did so within a few seconds. However, the outline of the creature remained attached to the figure of her father, like his own shadow!

Anukriti tried to scream out loud. However, her voice choked. The tears flowed relentlessly while her body shook in fear. Her father seemed to be a ghost. Yes, he appeared to be a monster's slave, who was luring her into his web of death.

Anukriti voicelessly uttered, 'Baba, I am scared. Please don't do this!'

The man remained unperturbed. He coldly eyed her and then came close to her. She felt paralyzed and was unable to move. He touched her fingers with his icy hand and then said in a stony voice, 'Come with me. I have come to take you...'

In that moment of sheer horror, Anukriti saw the man melt like lava and blend into the shadow behind him. It was a horrific sight and she was at her wits' end. Then the light flickered and like a magic spell, it was all gone. The horrific sequence of events unfolding in front of her eyes all vanished into thin air.

Anukriti was completely exhausted and before she fainted, or perhaps fell asleep out of trauma, she whispered, 'I love you, Baba...'

12 May 2017, 'Haunted Talks', Bandra, Mumbai, 7.10 p.m.

The Revelation

I was sitting on a small leather-cushioned stool on the small podium. The stage and the background curtains were black in colour, and so was the floor of the podium. In front of me was a full house; the audience were seated on black chairs inside the medium-sized yet cozy room designed specifically for stand-up shows. The lights were already dimmed and a spotlight illuminated me from above. Yes, I was in the spotlight for the first time.

Even though every aspect of that evening seemed to be tinged in darkness, I was confident that my words wouldn't be dark. My heart beat faster as I noticed the sparkle in the eyes of the folks seated close to the stage, right in front of me.

I clasped the mic with both my hands and began, 'Good evening, everyone! I am Jay Alani and I am a paranormal investigator. But let me be very clear, my identity is different from the popular connotations of the term "paranormal investigator". I am not here to catch ghosts or tell you flowery stories about demons and devils whom I have encountered. I strongly believe that I have a mission, and it is to eliminate blind faith. Across the world, and predominantly in our country, the belief system around ghosts and spirits is very gross. I find it very difficult to adhere to these beliefs which allow scammers to deceive innocent people.'

A murmur reverberated across the room, but I sensed that there was some confidence in it. I continued, 'Ghosts, wherever they might exist, were once humans too. Their realm needs to be respected. The definition of spirits, ghosts and the paranormal realm is not a simple one. I believe that it is something that doesn't need an explanation via what we consider logic. It is, in a way, the co-existence of both the residual and active energies that we are all made of. It is the unexplained truth behind a superpower that defines life as well. It is the journey of a mind full of questions, which compelled me to dive deep into the paranormal world. Being alive and being a ghost are so similar. We, as the advanced human race, don't have an explanation for either. Isn't it so?

So let us not speculate. I think mutual respect would make us understand the paranormal more deeply.'

I was feeling jittery, but I took a deep breath and then tried to focus. Looking at my audience, I said, 'First, let me apologize for cancelling the show earlier. It was supposed to be my first stand-up talk show in which I would tell everyone about myself and my work. However, even after bookings were confirmed, I cancelled the event. I am really sorry for that. But the reason for doing so was not something trivial. I needed to help somebody. Yes, I shall tell you about the case tonight.'

The silence within the room was deafening. The spotlight above me was dimmed a little, and the pupils of my eyes were dilated enough to see the faces of the people in front of me. I held the mic with my right hand and continued…

Two months ago, roughly three days before my first show here, I was sitting in my room and scrolling through social media when I clicked and opened Facebook Messenger. I confess that to this day, I am not very keen on using that particular chat platform. So most of the messages I receive on Facebook Messenger remain unopened.

It was about 11.00 in the night, and I skimmed through a couple of unread messages. Then I came upon one particular message whose last line read, 'Can you please help…'

The message was about three weeks old, and was from a girl named Anukriti. She had written, 'Hi Jay, my name is Anukriti and I am from Ahmedabad… There is something that has been troubling me lately and I want to talk to you about it. I know about you and your work. And my family and I desperately need your help. Can you please help…'

It was late at night, but a strange intuition created a feeling of uneasiness within me. I thought for a few seconds and then pinged back. I sent her my phone number and added the following message: 'Hi Anukriti. Call me back on this number. I will try to help you.'

Within ten minutes, my phone rang. I looked at my watch and saw that it was 11.25 p.m. Without any hesitation, I received the call and a soft feminine voice spoke from the other end, 'Hi Jay, I am Anukriti. Sorry for calling so late in the night. I just saw your message and couldn't stop myself from calling.'

There was a feel of anxiety in her voice and I assured her, 'It's all right, Anukriti. Now, please tell me what you want to discuss.'

Anukriti said grimly, 'I live in Ahmedabad with my mother. We are a family of four. My younger brother is a student and lives in Surat. I have recently completed my graduation and I am pursuing my post-graduate studies. My father, my Baba, is no more...'

A slight pause followed, and I realized that she was crying silently. Then she said, 'Jay, I think... I suspect that a haunting is happening in our house. Even as I am sitting on my bed and talking to you, I can feel it going on all around me!'

'Anukriti, tell me everything,' I said sceptically.

She replied, 'I can tell you the whole thing in short.'

'No,' I interrupted. 'I need to know the details so that I can help you. Tell me everything without any hesitation.'

Anukriti exhaled and then continued, 'Okay, I will try my best... Twelve years ago, we were a happy family of four. My baba was a businessman and my Maa was a housewife. I was a child and my brother was an infant. Baba was a doting father and I was his beloved pet. My brother and I were like the two chambers of his heart. But I knew I had a little extra place in that loving heart of his. Then one day, my Baba suffered huge losses in his business and became financially insolvent. It was a big jolt for him and he grew weak, both mentally and physically. Unable to find the means to improve the situation, he stopped going to work. I was too young to understand his ordeal. Then he started staying indoors almost throughout the day. He used to lock himself up inside his room for hours. Suddenly, he completely isolated himself from the outside world. Maa was scared, very scared. I could see her cry in despair. But in front of us, she pretended to be normal. Jay, it was such a distressing time, I just cannot explain the level of pain we felt as a family.'

I listened carefully as the silence of the night wrapped around me like a blanket. Anukriti said, 'Baba even stopped talking to us! He had his food sent to his own room and would eat all alone and remain locked within that same room for days! He seldom came out.'

Anukriti paused once again and I realized that she was gasping for breath as she spoke. She drank some water and continued, 'Then one day, he came out of his room to have dinner with us. We were overjoyed. Maa served us dinner and we sat together for the meal. Baba seemed all right, but still very nervous. As he ate, he said to us, "A shadowy spell of black magic has me in its grip. It is like a blanket that surrounds me all the time. I feel enclosed within the watertight grip of that evil spell. And that thing has brought with it a dark spirit to torture me! Oh, it's so ghastly! That demon is all around me. I can see its monstrous shadow inside my room! I cannot see my own shadow because it is eclipsed by the demon's silhouette. He laughs at me and points his fingers at me. He howls soundlessly but my eardrums explode with his hellish screams. The demon has consumed my entire existence and his uncanny embrace holds me as a prisoner wherever I go. I am broken and I am scared that this demon will try to harm my family, my little children... I just cannot let this happen! I live with this demon all the time but I cannot let it torment you. So I have distanced myself from everybody. Please try to understand where I am coming from. I am fighting a battle that I cannot afford to lose."'

Anukriti was in tears as she spoke, 'We cried profusely that night. Maa was absolutely helpless. I tried to hug Baba, but he almost ran away and locked himself up in his room again! He remained there for days, and we could only hear his never-ending, otherworldly sobs that tore our hearts apart. We were totally dependent on Maa and she was broken too. Her heart was shattered but she tried her best to make both ends meet. My maternal uncle, our family physician and other relatives tried their best to help. They even tried to get medical help for Baba. Alas, nothing worked... Then, one morning, Maa went into his room with his tea and stood horrorstruck! Her scream struck me like an electric shock and I ran in. Baba was not on his bed. He had hanged himself from the ceiling! His lifeless body was hanging in front of our eyes! Aaaahhh...it was such a horrific blow! We reeled from its impact for months.'

She added in a grim voice, 'As time passed, Maa took care of us and the family. She took a job and her earnings financially supported us. But I know that deep within, she believed what Baba had said. She believed that the evil spirit was indeed there. She never forgot that fateful incident. She believed what he said before dying.'

It was painful to listen to her story but I remained patient and calm. Then I asked her, 'Anukriti, I know how shattering the incident must have been, but it happened 12 years ago. Tell me, what is troubling you at present? How is this related to the hauntings you told me about?'

Anukriti answered, 'Right now, my brother is at my maternal uncle's place in Surat. He is in secondary school. Maa and I still live in our own house where Baba passed away. Yes, Jay, it has been 12 years, but for the last two months, I have been going through the same thing as Baba.'

My heart skipped a beat and I said, 'What do you mean? How?'

Anukriti replied, 'Jay, I think Baba's spirit has not departed. Perhaps it still lives among us, in this house. Maybe his soul has returned for a reason, or maybe it couldn't exit this mortal world. Jay, I am sure. Yes, I am! His soul, and that demonic spirit that killed him, are still locked inside that same room. They never left us.'

She sounded terrified as she spoke. 'You know, I never told this to anybody. In all these 12 years, I have always felt their presence in our house. Both Maa and I, at times, had an uncanny feeling that they were close by.'

I interrupted her and said, 'Anukriti, this is a common phenomenon as far as human emotions are concerned. After a traumatic incident, people sometimes get such feelings. Don't be frightened of them.'

'I know, Jay,' she replied. 'But this is different. For the last two months, I can sense it more intensely than ever. The uncanny feeling is so powerful. Something or somebody is in this house. And it is inside this house. I know it is Baba. He is here! A negative force has taken over my entire life all of a sudden. My life was moving smoothly, but now it is full to the brim with this negativity. I have been in a stable relationship with my boyfriend, but despite the fact that I still love him, I have ended our relationship for no rhyme or reason. My life has become more negative with every passing moment. I don't

feel like meeting anyone or talking to anybody. My whole life is suddenly a mess. Jay, I have consulted doctors and counsellors but nothing helped.'

Anukriti sounded helpless as she said, 'Jay, I really don't know why it's happening, but everything I said is true. I feel so hopeless. I know somebody is shadowing me. I don't know if it is depression or the lack thereof that is giving me these horrific nightmares that don't let me sleep! And I am drawn to the room where Baba died, as if a magnet is pulling me in that direction. I spend hours there, not knowing why, and sit there idly. Jay, I think…no, I know Baba has come back, and the demon has followed him too. He has come to take me with him!'

Anukriti's voice suddenly grew shriller as she added, 'To end the negativity, I can die and be with my Baba because I love him and he loves me a lot. I just want to ensure that it's Baba and not the demon who wants me. I would love to go with Baba… Jay, I need your help to know the truth.'

A profound silence followed, and in that moment I made up my mind. 'She needs my help urgently! I need to go. Yes, I have to go, or else an innocent girl will die.'

So I cancelled my last show and went ahead to fight an invisible battle with the paranormal…

The Flashback: Mid-Year 2015, and the Year that Followed, Mumbai

The snake-bite at Vasai Fort was a painful one, but what followed the accident was worse. Despite taking anti-venom injections, the wound was festering. The Vasai Fort case was my first professional investigation in Mumbai and I was desperate.

In that desperation, I became reckless and unmindful and that led me into the accident. Sadly, I didn't have much money and I needed funds to buy expensive medicines to treat my wound.

As I realized that I wouldn't be able to manage the costs of my treatment, I reached out to Baba and Priyanka for some help. It was becoming more difficult for me to survive and stay afloat in Mumbai with every passing day. I had consulted three doctors and each one of them prescribed medicines that I couldn't afford.

Baba extended a helping hand and added, 'Jay, haven't you had enough now? This unrealistic dream will lead you nowhere! Discard your experiments and come home.'

Priyanka sent me some money and said, 'This is too dangerous a profession! It is not only financially unviable but also a threat to your own life! Give it up, dear, and come back. Something must have worked out by now if it was ever meant to happen. Try to understand and stop!'

I was in no mood to listen to these moral lectures and sent them both rude replies. I knew they were hurt by my behaviour, but I was really determined to prove my worth. The snake-bite led to one more complication. As my body weakened, I had to discontinue the food-cart business, and thus lost a means to earn whatever little money I was making. Hence, under the yoke of penury, I visited pharmacies to purchase cheaper alternatives to the medicines that were prescribed to me. I was really broken but my hope was still alive.

Thankfully, with the money that I borrowed from Baba and Priyanka, I found a good doctor in Andheri, purchased proper medicines, and about a week later, my wound healed. However, during my visits to Andheri, I realized that I was unnecessarily hurting myself by living in Naigaon. I had the option to find cheap accommodation somewhere in Andheri, Juhu or Lokhandwala where the offices of prospective production houses were located. Once again, I my finances were in a really bad shape, and none of the production houses had shown any interest in my pitches. So, by reducing the need to undertake hectic commutes to Andheri every day and continue my struggle, I could at least take care of my deteriorating health. I used some real estate apps to find a paying guest (PG) accommodation. I had to shamelessly borrow some money from a few friends once again.

A few days later, I touched base with a few guys who were looking for a roommate for a PG accommodation. The rent was just ₹2,000 a month. Without any further delay, I accepted their offer. Alas, I didn't know then what awaited me there.

As I moved into the old building with my little luggage, I saw that there were seven people who were crammed inside a 250-square-foot (or maybe a little larger) room in that PG accommodation. And I was the eighth person to join them! The rent for the whole place was ₹16,000 and was supposed to be divided into eight equal portions.

The place was really bad. It was pathetic! Everyone slept on mattresses laid on the floor. There was no furniture in the room. It was empty. But the presence of too many human beings made the air claustrophobic. Alas, I didn't have any options, so I went to live in that abyss. For weeks and months, I only survived on bread, boiled eggs and instant noodles. It was a horrible period of my life. Some of the guys even managed to cook inside that miniscule space just to save a bit of money! It was painful for all of us.

Six of my roommates were struggling actors who would wake up at 6.00 a.m. to go to the gym. In the commotion of their morning activities, I couldn't even sleep properly after staying up late with my work—making presentations and drafting emails to be sent to prospective production houses. Life was becoming tougher by the day, and in that dingy place, I was losing myself in unending circles of phone-calls, meetings, emails and then hopelessness! Maybe such content, the kind that I was conceptualizing, was not viable in the Indian media ecosystem. However, the way they handed out rejections was both rude and uncertain. I had to sleep alongside that crowd of people whose dreams, like mine, were failing—I began to hate my life!

Then one day, I got a response. It was from a man named Mr Suhail Mathur from Big Magic Studios. He politely asked me to meet him at his office. It was a positive response and I held on to it.

The next day, I reached the venue and went in. I was seated inside a meeting room of the corporate office and my heart began to beat faster. Then the door opened and a man came in. He was a tall, handsome, well-dressed and well-behaved person with a smile on his face. He had an aura of positivity and I felt relieved.

He shook hands with me and sat down. Then he began the conversation, 'Hi, I am Suhail Mathur. I read your proposal and I was fascinated by the idea you have shared. Can you tell me more?'

That was the moment when I poured my heart out. I began, 'I am Jay Alani and I am a paranormal investigator. But unlike scammers who boast of crusading against ghosts and demons with hi-tech gadgets, I have created a simple mission for myself. It is to eliminate blind faith and uphold paranormal reality.'

Suhail's eyes grew brighter and I found a great listener in him. That meeting went on for two and a half hours and I told him everything. I don't know why, but I sensed that he trusted me. I told him everything—my family, my insecurities, my love, my dream, my struggle and my unending hope. He was the first person to trust me. He showed me that I had some worth but I needed to choose the right path to explore it.

At the end of the meeting, I knew I had found a new friend and a guide in this man. Suhail said, 'Jay, continue to dream because that is what keeps us alive. I am happy that you've chosen something radical. Even though the media might not recognize it now, one day they will definitely do so. I will be glad to help you out.'

Thus, days passed and I saw our bond grow stronger. I was a mere struggler whom everyone ignored. Now I was like family to Suhail, who had an established career and was the proud founder of a flourishing literary agency. Yet he recognized my worth and I felt confident. I connected to people via Suhail, and even went to attend a literary festival in Lonavla. I gained immense confidence as, for the first time, I could tell my stories to an audience. I was really happy.

Suhail even invited me to his place on several occasions. His spouse, the charming Sumedha Mathur, was a lady of substance, who showered her warmth, friendship and love on me. In their family, I became a perpetual friend who would often barge in for an animated chat over dinner.

On one such night, as I was coming back from Suhail's house, I got into a shared cab. The other passenger was a woman in her mid-thirties. She was a bright young woman who was decently dressed in corporate attire, and was perhaps returning home from work.

Her name was Shilpa and she sat on the backseat while I took the front seat. As we drove, a formal introduction followed and I mentioned that I was a struggling paranormal investigator. She got excited about my profession and we talked for a while. Then we got off the cab and went inside a coffee shop, and for the next one and a half hours, I told her many things about my own experiences.

'Jay, I am an event manager for stand-up comedians. I arrange shows for them,' said Shilpa. 'I book their venues, organize the logistics and get a commission on ticket sales.'

She looked at me and said with confidence, 'Why don't you start a stand-up show on horror? I am sure that such a show would be immensely popular among people! A talk show with a real-life paranormal investigator is a unique idea! People would love to hear about you and your investigations. Now, listen. This Sunday, let us experiment with this idea! Let's do a show at Bandra. What do you think?'

I was completely speechless but I was feeling elated. She added, 'Whatever we earn from ticket sales, we shall split. After paying for the venue and the logistics, you will take 80 per cent and I will take 20 per cent.'

I was on cloud nine! I said, 'Yes! Let's do it! And I would call the show "Haunted Talks" by Jay Alani…'

We exchanged phone numbers and went back to our respective homes. It was a day of positives—the day Jay Alani got himself back.

As I sat inside my cluttered room, surrounded by my roommates, I saw the show go live on BookMyShow. And then I received the message from Anukriti. I pinged her my phone number and quietly went out of the room and climbed up to the rooftop. I knew that the phone would soon start to ring. A new case had already arrived.

April 2017, Rabari Colony, Ahmedabad

The 'Demon' Unveiled

Everything I said during my first live show of 'Haunted Talks' was true—it was the actual account of an experience that was as horrific as it was emotional. Yet what Anukriti experienced was extremely turbulent. It is easy to speak about a painful incident that happens over a few months or even years. Each day, with every passing minute, brought the same amount of torment.

Anukriti said to me during the call as she sobbed like a child, 'Jay, I am afraid to sleep. Nowadays, just as I close my eyes and try to sleep, nightmares attack me! Last night, I saw my Baba's hanging body, and as I got closer, his eyes flew open and I saw a fiery gleam in them. It was so ghostly! His gaping mouth called my name in a strange voice, while froth dripped from his lips. Ohh…it was horrific. Then, he stretched his hands towards me and I screamed in horror! I woke up immediately, and I sat there and perspired like a victim of extreme distress.'

She added, 'This was not the only occasion when I experienced such a torment. A few days ago, I saw him in my dream. He was sitting in front of me. I was on my bed and he was beside me. As I looked around, I noticed that I was not in my own room. I was in Baba's room and I was sitting on his bed. I looked back and saw his face. It was grim and quiet. And then, suddenly it began to change. Like magic, it changed into the mutilated face of a devilish monster, whose eyes were like burning lumps of coal and whose skin was scaly! His tongue was like that of a serpent, and it stretched towards me to grasp me! That night, too, I woke up in a state of frenzy and was unable to sleep.'

'Anukriti, calm down,' I said. 'Such tormenting dreams often haunt people. Just try to think about happy things…'

However, she interrupted me and said, 'These are not just dreams. Jay, these are real. Each night, as my nightmares end and I sit on my bed, I can see a huge shadow of a demon. It slowly surrounds me and then engulfs me in an embrace. Then it whispers in Baba's familiar voice and says, "*Anukriti, my dear, the time has come. I have come for you…*" Jay, please help me. Please tell me that it is Baba who will take me, and will not hurt me! Isn't it so? Please!'

That telephonic conversation with Anukriti lasted two long hours. As I listened to her, I felt completely drained. My heart was full of questions. '*Why does destiny deliver such painful blows on people? A happy family got shattered within such a small period. And now this young girl is at her wits' end. No, I can't sit back after hearing everything. I must do something!*'

I took a deep breath, and said with determination, 'Anukriti, don't panic. I am coming to Ahmedabad. Yes, I will come to help you. Just wait for me. I will come quickly.'

As I disconnected the call, I reclined on my bed. My spine was hurting and my head was throbbing. I knew it was a singular case and a very special one. I closed my eyes to take some rest.

The next morning, I woke up to prepare for my journey, but I had no clue as to how I would do so. I didn't even have enough money to sustain myself in Mumbai for too long. How could I go to Ahmedabad? But I had to do something desperate because I was not ready to let Anukriti die. I had to meet her personally and dive deep into her subconscious mind to understand what was happening, and then frame a modus operandi to help her. According to her, the demon was back and had her father's soul as its captive slave! I had to wage a war against the paranormal force.

Out of this compulsion to help a victim, I took my lone laptop and sold it off at just ₹9,000. With the money I received, I bought a train ticket to Ahmedabad and reached there within a couple of days. I checked into a local motel near the station. The room was supposed to cost me ₹600 per night, but it still seemed too expensive to me. With an overgrown beard and a mass of unkempt hair, I looked distraught and haggard like a vagabond. I dropped off my luggage, took a quick shower, and called Anukriti to note down her address.

Then I headed towards Anukriti's house in Rabari Colony.

Theirs was a small, one-storey house. I entered and rang the doorbell. Soon a lady in her late fifties came out and opened the gate. She was Anukriti's mother Mrs Shukla Shah. She welcomed me inside and I noticed that there was a motherly affection in her nature.

As we sat in the living room, Anukriti came out and sat beside me. She was a beautiful young girl with long black hair and large expressive eyes. In a simple salwar suit, she carried herself gracefully, which made her seem even prettier. Yet I could notice a tortured shadow over her face that covered it like a dark veil. It seemed to eclipse her charming personality.

As we talked, I realized that both Anukriti and Mrs Shukla Shah were aware of the things that were happening around them. Anukriti was visibly happy to see me. Then I asked, 'Can I see the room? I mean your Baba's room.'

She nodded her head and the three of us got up. We went past the kitchen and came in front of a door. Anukriti opened it and we went inside. Within the room, there was a bed, a cupboard and a small wooden table with a chair. For a moment, Anukriti looked up at the ceiling and then looked down. I noticed it and understood that the point from where the electric fan hung reminded her of her father's suicide. I chose not to say anything.

Anukriti and her mother sat down on the bed and I sat on the chair. I wanted them to trust me, and let them feel that I believed in their convictions. For a few minutes, there was complete silence and I waited patiently.

Then Anukriti said, 'Jay, this is where I spend most of my time now. I sit on this bed as if drawn by a magnet, and wait for my fate. Everything I told you is true. Last night, I slept in this room. Maa didn't want me to do it, but I couldn't control it. I had to be here. All night long, the shadow emerged out of it and locked me in its vice-like grip! I felt suffocated as my heart sought an answer.'

'Wait,' I interrupted. 'You just said that the shadow emerged out of "it". What is it?'

Anukriti stood up and opened the cupboard. She took out something and held it in her hands. It was an old photograph of a little girl sitting on a man's lap. She said, 'This is a photo of Baba and me. It was clicked on my tenth birthday. I was so happy that day. I found this in his cupboard the day he passed away. Ever since then, I have let it remain here. Now when I sit alone here on this bed, I hold it close to my bosom to draw some strength from it. But for the last few days, the shadow, with that harrowing voice and mutilated face, emerges out of it and surrounds me. It summons me to my end. Jay, I think Baba is held captive by that demon. He is his slave now! They are here to take me and I…'

She paused a bit and said in a choking voice, 'I can go with Baba, if he really wants that…'

In that instant, my eyes met those of Mrs Shah and I understood that she wanted to say something to me. She was under a lot of stress and was perspiring.

The atmosphere within the room was damp and scary, and then, something happened. Mrs Shukla abruptly interrupted and said, 'Anukriti, my child, Jay has just arrived after a long journey. He looks famished. Dear, we shall tell him everything and I trust his abilities. But first, please go to Festive Restaurant and fetch him some food.'

She turned towards me and added, 'Please accept my apologies, I haven't cooked anything for you. Please excuse her for an hour. She will come back really quickly!'

Her voice had a decisive and overbearing quality that surprised both Anukriti and me. However, Anukriti got up like an obedient girl and went out. Before she left, she placed the photograph on the bed and took another quick look at the ceiling.

I turned towards her mother and saw an earnest urge in her eyes that seemed to say silently, 'Please, let her go for a while. I need to tell you something.'

I nodded my head in agreement. As Anukriti went out, Mrs Shukla and I started talking. Her voice was marked by intense terror. Outside the house, a wedding procession danced along the adjacent road. And our own voices drowned in the loud noise of the blaring loudspeakers.

Then, Anukriti returned about 45 minutes later. She kept the food packets on the dining table and stepped into the room—her Baba's room—where we were still anxiously awaiting her. As she entered and sat on the bed, her eyes searched for something. I followed her gaze and realized the real reason behind her anxiety. Surprisingly and strangely, the photograph had suddenly vanished from the bed and none of us had any clue where it was!

It was a truly scary moment and I realized that the devil was slowly getting unveiled.

November 2017, Mumbai

A Ray of Hope

Did Anukriti's story end on a positive note or did she get consumed by the demon? Well, I shall tell you everything.

Almost six or seven months after that incident, when I had abandoned all hopes of living in Bandra, I shifted base again and moved to an apartment in Andheri. This time, I landed an opportunity to work as an assistant director with the help of some independent producers. I even worked on voice-overs. I wrote for those shows and began to make some money. With this money, I paid two months' rent as an initial deposit and shifted to a new apartment which was a solo accommodation.

Alas, that didn't end my sufferings and destiny had more pain in store for me. The little work that had just begun to come along stopped suddenly. It was a time when I felt completely lost and didn't have anywhere to go. Then something else happened.

One evening, as I sat in my apartment, I kept wondering how I would survive financially. I stood near the little window of my room and cried, 'Why is the world so cruel? None of the meetings I attended ever ended on a negative note. But they never led to anything either! Why do people ask for project proposals when they don't have any intention of doing anything with those projects? So they keep on postponing their decisions! They don't understand that these delays not only destroy people's aspirations but also murder their dreams. I am afraid that the ghosts of these murdered dreams will one day overcrowd the paranormal world!'

The sun had already set and the sky above was clear. Millions of stars twinkled in it and I looked at them in search of a miracle that would save my own dreams from dying.

The phone rang, disrupting my reverie.

'Hi Jay! This is Suhail,' said the person on the other end. 'I have something urgent to discuss and I need to meet you. Tomorrow is Sunday, so can you come down to my place around 5.00 p.m.? I want you to meet somebody. I will tell you the details tomorrow when we meet.'

My heart thumped in my chest and I agreed. I couldn't sleep the entire night. The next evening, I reached Suhail's apartment at the appointed time and rang the doorbell. Sumedha opened the door and welcomed me. She had always been a warm host and a kind woman. I stepped inside and saw two people seated on the sofa. One was Suhail and the other person was a stranger. However, I got positive vibes from his pleasant appearance and calm smile.

As I sat on the sofa, Suhail introduced us, saying, 'Hi Jay, this is Mr Neil D'Silva. He is a fantastic author. He has written several successful English books in the horror genre.

And, Neil, this is Jay Alani, the man with a mission! Jay is a paranormal investigator and is on a no-nonsense drive to uphold paranormal reality, and uproot blind faith.'

I was surprised that Suhail remembered so much about me—a man who was yet to prove anything! My respect for him grew manifold. He continued, 'You know, Neil, Jay's work isn't easy. It is really tough to survive as an honest paranormal investigator without resorting to gimmicks. However, he has some very interesting stories to tell. The intriguing cases that he has investigated are really worth talking about…'

Suhail turned to me and said, 'Jay, Neil's journey has not been simple either. He has struggled a lot to fulfil his dreams. Despite being a father of two little kids, he chose to quit his established business and become a full-time author. However, gaining financial stability by becoming a successful author of Indian horror is something that is yet to become a feasible option in our country. Well, with the support of his wife, Neil could take this courageous step forward. They are a brave couple and I respect them for that…'

Sumedha came in with coffee and snacks. She sat with us and said with a smile, 'So that means we have two heroes in our house this evening! This feels so special. I think the two of you complement each other in your bid to do something radical.'

Suhail added, 'Yes, and that is exactly why I have invited the two of you. Let us collaborate and create a book! It would be a non-fiction book on Indian horror. It would be about the real-life paranormal investigations conducted by Jay Alani, and written by the very talented and prolific best-selling author Neil D'Silva. Guys, trust me, this would become a blockbuster that would redefine Indian literary culture! Let us do this. My literary agency, The Book Bakers, would pitch this book and I am more than confident that an A-list publisher would take it up.'

My eyes glittered with hope and I saw the same in Neil's eyes as we shook hands. Thus we took the first step towards the realization of the book that we co-authored. It was represented by The Book Bakers team. I didn't know, and I guess neither did Neil, that what we were undertaking would eventually become a true literary bestseller published by an elite international publisher.

I looked at Suhail and asked, 'What shall we name this book?'

He looked at both of us for a moment and just then, like a striking coincidence, the lights went out. It was a power cut.

While we sat there in the darkness, with only the dim glow of the moonlight entering through the open window, Suhail smirked eerily and replied, 'We would name it "HAUNTED"!'

12 May 2017, 'Haunted Talks', Bandra, Mumbai

The 'Tale' Continues...

A shroud of silence had fallen over the audience as they listened to the tale I was relating. Yet it was not just a story. It was an incident that had actually happened. The clock reminded me that we had been in conversation for over one and a half hours.

I drank some water and began…

The evening I received Anukriti's first message and spoke with her over the phone was very special. Good things were happening in my life after a very long time. That night, at around 10.30 p.m., the bookings for my first show had gone live on BookMyShow. It was supposed to be my first live event and I was super happy. I had even updated my social media profiles and tagged many people as well. But then, the Anukriti episode happened, and I made up my mind. Within the next couple of days, as I told you, I was in Ahmedabad. Yes, it was the very Sunday on which my show was supposed to happen. Gathering some courage, I called Shilpa and requested her if the show could be postponed.

At first, Shilpa was completely shocked as the tickets for the show were almost sold out. However, I explained everything to her and she understood. I am ever thankful to her for her patience with me and my mission. Hence, after so many months, I am able to sit here and tell you Anukriti's story.

So as we came to terms with the shocking disappearance of the photograph, I said, 'Let us go out of here.'

Once we were out of the room, I looked at the two of them and said, 'I am here in Ahmedabad just for you. Yes, Anukriti. I am here because I want to offer my support as a paranormal investigator. But unfortunately, I don't have the means to support myself financially. I don't know how long I need to stay here, but I really cannot afford it.'

I turned towards Mrs Shukla and pleaded, 'Ma'am, I know it sounds crazy, but can you let me stay in your house? I simply need a room in this house. I know that I am a complete stranger and you might feel sceptical about my intentions. But I am really helpless and shamelessly asking for this favour.'

Mrs Shukla interrupted me and said, 'No, Jay. I don't think of you as a stranger anymore. You have volunteered to help me save my daughter. I will be glad to be your host.'

Maybe she was a bit sceptical but she didn't reveal that

explicitly. I was her only hope. For the next eight days, I stayed in that house. Yes, I lived there as a part of their family. And maybe, unknowingly, I made a place for myself in their hearts.

I told Anukriti, 'The only way to drive away the negative energy is to create more and more positive energy. The entity that has showered darkness over this house needs to be overcome through the light of courage.'

Thus from that moment, we refrained from speaking about the paranormal and spent our days trading good vibes. Mrs Shukla accepted my request and took a week-long leave from work. Together, we visited shopping malls, watched movies, ate our meals and had a lot of fun. Within such a little time, I became their friend. Yes, I became Anukriti's friend…or maybe something more.

We used to chat for hours and speak about everything. We used to stay up late at night. At times, we would go to sleep at 2.00 a.m.! Surrounded by my newfound family and a blossoming friendship, I forgot my own griefs. Yes, I felt happy and cried tears of joy as I went to sleep at night.

Despite everything, I still noticed a blankness in Anukriti's eyes. An unanswered question persisted behind her pupils. It was a question that I could decipher and my heart would sink every time: 'What will happen next? Where is that photograph? Will the demon overpower Baba's spirit to take my soul away? I don't want to die!'

Then something happened on a fateful evening.

Anukriti and I were sitting on the sofa in the living room as Mrs Shukla prepared dinner in the kitchen which was adjacent to the living room. I got up to get my phone from my room and as I returned and sat down, Anukriti screamed, 'Jay, what is that?'

Mrs Shukla and I were jolted by the shock in her voice

and turned around. Anukriti was staring at her Baba's room. We were taken by surprise to see that something was burning inside the room. We immediately hurried to the room and stood near the door to see what was going on. Amidst a pile of old newspapers, the photograph of Anukriti and her Baba was on fire! We stood like statues as everything burnt to ashes within a few minutes. Anukriti was shaking as she cried profusely. She looked at me and howled, 'Jay! No, this can't be! It was my fondest memory of my Baba! It's gone now. How, Jay? How?'

At that moment, I turned towards her and said sternly, 'I have set it on fire!'

Anukriti looked at me and shuddered. Then she wailed out loud, 'Jay, what have you done? I can never get it back! I feel so lonely. Ahhhh, I am so alone...'

I held her hand and took her to the sofa. I made her sit down. None of us spoke and there was complete silence in the room. When her nerves calmed down a bit, I said, 'Anukriti, this was necessary. I have burnt the demon. It was living inside that cursed photograph. That devilish dark spirit is gone and so is...'

Anukriti cried out, 'No, Jay! You didn't do the right thing!'

I placed my finger on her lips and silenced her. Then I took out something from under the table and placed it in her hands. It was a copy of the same photograph!

Anukriti looked at it and her expression changed like magic. She lovingly kissed the photograph several times and then...she hugged me! Yes, she hugged me like a child and wept. 'Thank you for all the love!'

As that moment remained etched in time, I also became speechless. Was there music in the air? I don't know. Was it a budding romance or just innocent love? I don't know. Then what was it? Maybe it was a moment that celebrated the victory of happiness and the joy of being alive.

Anukriti was never a victim of a 'paranormal haunting'. She was a victim of a serious mental condition that is known as 'post-traumatic stress disorder' or PTSD.

Yes, she was suffering from the strange illness and she needed serious help. Right from the first day, I knew that she was not a victim of a haunting. It was a clear case of PTSD, triggered by the trauma of her father's death. I knew I needed to convince her that her Baba had not come back to take her. And it was my biggest challenge! The hormone oxytocin is normally produced in the hypothalamus inside the brain, and is released by the pituitary. It plays a significant role in social bonding, reproduction, childbirth, and the period after childbirth. In common terms, it is also referred to as the 'love hormone'. Deep trauma messes with our oxytocin levels, and causes hallucinations and symptoms of mental health conditions. Such conditions are often very painful and serious. This hormone controls emotions such as empathy, love and trust. Following a traumatic event, a person can suffer from conditions of unidentified and unrevealed stress that secretly alter their oxytocin levels. The victims are often unaware of these changes that are revealed several years later in the form of mental health conditions such as phantasms. Anukriti needed medical help to overcome the condition. I did my best to help her and present her with a normal life.

That evening, she wept for almost 30 minutes. I sat there quietly. Then she stopped and wiped away her tears. She looked at me and I spoke. 'Anukriti, the day I came to your house and your Maa sent you to get some food, I listened to her confession very carefully. She understood that you were in pain and needed help. She never believed that you were a victim of a haunting, either. But she didn't have the answers to your questions. That evening, as we discussed, I made a phone call to a very senior psychiatrist in Delhi, whom I knew. He is a 73-year-old doctor and a genius. He told me so much and guided me. He gave me a different perspective. I realized that you needed the blanket of a warm relationship of love and compassion. You needed to talk to somebody about everything… And then you needed to go for proper medication.'

Anukriti cried again. She didn't know that she was suffering from a strange mental illness. We were sitting near the window and a light breeze tousled her beautiful hair. She touched my hands and said in a shaky voice, 'Jay… I miss Baba. I miss him a lot. Deep down, I now know that I have been dreaming all of it up. Whatever I saw was a product of my own imagination. Baba cannot be a ghost! He loved me. He can never be a demon's slave or try to kill me! How can a doting father kill his own daughter? That is impossible. Even if the dark spirit that took his life tries to kill me, I won't let that happen!'

'There is no dark spirit here,' I interrupted. 'Your loneliness augmented your mental helplessness. You were never a victim of any haunting. That evening, I removed the photograph myself. I am sorry but I needed to do it. Then I secretly got it photocopied. Today, I lit that fire when I went to fetch my phone. This stupid drama was necessary. Yes, it was necessary to discard the fears within you! But now you have overcome it. I am happy. Anukriti, I am really happy.'

A smile appeared on her face and she hugged me again for almost a minute. Then we laughed together. It was an emotional moment and we felt happy.

I asked her, 'Anukriti, will you come with me and meet a doctor? I want you to complete a course of medication that would help you. Will you do that for me? Or I should say, will you do that for your Baba?'

She nodded and smiled. I felt relieved. Mrs Shukla smiled, perhaps after many days. We had dinner together and the day ended on a positive note.

Anukriti was very lonely. It was true. From Mrs Shukla's words, I gathered that Anukriti's boyfriend was a non-serious guy who just wanted to fool around with her and have fun. He never cared about her emotions and there was no foundation of love between them. Thus their breakup was inevitable. Alas, inadvertently, it augmented her elusive grief.

So unfortunately, in the absence of her mother or anyone else to talk to, she couldn't share her feelings fully. Though her trauma originated in her early childhood, her PTSD revealed itself in her youth. In such a complex situation, she didn't know how to overcome it.

Yes, Anukriti did meet the doctor and took medicines. And now she has completely recovered and leads a normal life!

Friends, almost 95 per cent of all paranormal hauntings are just mental health issues in disguise. My mission as a paranormal investigator is to eliminate all blind faith and establish the reality of the paranormal world. I am happy that I could do so in Anukriti's case.

Thank you for listening to me so patiently, and for supporting me. Today's Haunted Talk ends now, but I promise I shall return with more such sessions!

As the show ended and the spotlight grew dim, I got up from my chair and walked down from the podium. Everyone around me stood up and clapped their hands. My eyes were already full of tears.

That evening of my first 'Haunted Talk' will always remain special for me. So would the case of Anukriti. Maybe Anukriti's Baba was also a victim of some mental health issue. Had somebody been able to help him, he wouldn't have lost his life! Across the world, every year, more people die from suicide triggered by such ailments than in military combats. It's extremely unfortunate.

Anukriti is now happily married and lives in Surat with her husband. A beautiful relationship gradually blossomed between Anukriti, Mrs Shukla and me that I shall cherish forever.

Well, even though I didn't dig out a daunting ghost during that investigation, I am happy that I could sustain my mission to uphold paranormal reality.

4

A Demon Inside

We are our own 'angel' and our own 'demon'.

March 2018, Dwarka, 5.45 p.m.

The Message Arrives

'Hi Jay, my name is Shalini and I am about to die! The demon is here to take away my soul!'

It was between 5.30 and 6.00 p.m. I casually looked at my computer screen as I scanned through the messages in my Facebook inbox. As I scrolled through a few regular ones, I was forced to pause when I saw one particular message. It was an unusual message and I froze on reading the opening line.

It was a random message from a girl named Shalini. I had an intense uncanny feeling as soon as I read her message. I clicked the link and went through the entire message.

Shalini: 'Yes…what you are reading is true!'

Shalini: 'I am at my wits' end and must surrender to the demon's quest for a soul—to complete this demonic game.'

Shalini: 'I am a student of dentistry and I live in Yamuna Nagar, Haryana.'

Shalini: 'The apparition haunting me floats around me even as I type these messages. I can feel its breath and hear its whispers, asking me to cut open my throat. I am scared and am on the brink of perishing!'

Shalini: 'For the last time, I want to talk to you and tell you my story. I have reached a point where I want to end my own life. Can you please help me out?'

August 2017, Mumbai, Midnight

A Choking Dilemma

Questions, questions and more questions!

By then my mind was totally overwhelmed by thoughts about where my fate was leading me. The dreams with which I had arrived in Mumbai started to crumble. The contradiction between my visions and the treatment they received from prospective patrons amazed me! Perhaps I was wrong. Perhaps the world of television media was still not ready to showcase the escapades of a paranormal investigator who strived to uphold paranormal reality instead of highlighting scary fables about ghosts!

The devil within my own soul was strong enough to consume me with a glaring fury. No angel had the strength to save me. In that tussle, I could hear the voice of the devil, '*I will come out soon! You can't stop me for much longer. The day is not far off when I will rise like an active volcano and consume your dreams!*'

I was gradually going insane with the frustration of not doing anything concrete.

'*Jay, this directionless voyage has no destination,*' I screamed at myself. '*Stop being stubborn. It's time for you to sit back and think about what needs to be done. The suffering doesn't need to be prolonged. Do something about it.*'

I stood in front of the mirror and looked at myself. In front of me stood a fatigued guy, with unkempt hair, a withered body, and a dry face with darkening eyes. I was shocked at the sight of my own state. What have I done to myself? Where will I end up if this ordeal continues?

It was a moment of retrospection for me and I stood speechless while I scrutinized every inch of my own body. I didn't feel any pity. I just felt a sudden rush of anger!

'*I don't want to return unless I have proved myself!*' I replied stubbornly.

'*Then so be it! Are you ready for the Armageddon?*' my subconscious devil screeched.

'*I don't know....*' Was my involuntary response.

With a flurry of reminiscences, the world of my love unfolded before my eyes.

That evening in December 2004 shall forever remain etched in my memory. I was just 18 and had returned from boarding school. Life in Patna was very different from the life I had spent in the hostel. My father had been in the business of civil construction work and my family was quite well-to-do. In the year 2004, we shifted to a newly built apartment. Our home was on the sixth floor of the building.

A subtle solitude always suffused my consciousness and I was a perpetually shy boy. During the evening, I found it tough to pass the time. So I chose to visit the rooftop where every evening the passionate kids of the building engaged in various activities. I used to stand by the parapet and watch them. However, most evenings, I just stood and observed the beautiful sunset on the western horizon.

It was on one such lazy winter evening that I saw her. She stood by an adjacent parapet and was chatting with a friend. Her radiant face, her sparkling smile, her innocent demeanour merged into an aura that overwhelmed me! I stood at my favourite corner and stared at her with awestruck eyes. It was a moment that was pre-decided by destiny, and I must say… I fell in love!

Yet I couldn't gather the courage to approach her. My introverted nature prevented me from doing anything. She was our neighbour who lived in the apartment on the fourth floor.

It took me a couple of days to gather enough courage and then, on a Sunday evening, as she stood alone, I went ahead and stood beside her. I felt nervous but remained determined, and struggled to conjure a smile on my face.

The smile broke the ice, and she smiled back. I blurted out, 'Hi, I am Jay and I live on the sixth floor. We moved into our new apartment two months ago.'

She looked into my eyes carelessly and replied, 'Hi Jay, I am Priyanka.'

In that brief rendezvous, I sensed that she was much shier that I was. Our conversation was momentary but felt ethereal.

Thus began our rooftop trysts every evening. A sweet friendship developed between us. She was a couple of years younger than me. She was very focused on her career. She wanted to become a doctor. Whereas I was actually clueless about what I would do in life! I only knew that I needed to become a civil engineer so that I could do justice to the legacy of my father's business.

I don't know when, but in the course of the vibrant hours that we spent together, the bond between us grew deeper. I knew that sparks were flying between us.

Soon I left Patna for an ill-fated stint at an engineering college where I struggled and failed miserably, only to return to Patna three years later. Baba was shattered by my failure, but he gradually came to realize that I was never meant to become an engineer.

In those three years, much had changed. Priyanka, along with her family, had shifted to another house. Thus our meetings became infrequent. Despite that, she helped me cope with the dejection of failure, and encouraged me to move ahead.

Yet that time, too, was short-lived. Then she shifted to Kota for her future education. On reaching Kota, she called me and I carefully noted down her number. Then began another period of desperation in my life as I began to owe more and more money at the various PCO booths from where I called her daily. The long trail of bills was like the slick tongue of a famished dragon whose hunger I somehow managed to appease. Finally, with my depleting pocket money, I bought a pair of small 'Reliance India Mobile' cellular phones which were popular at the time (primarily because they offered free calls between users of the same network). One I kept for myself, while the other I placed in a beautiful gift-box and mailed it to her, along with a heartfelt letter and some chocolates.

It was July 2007 and I received her call on my phone. As she started the conversation, I abruptly stopped her. In a sudden rush of adrenaline, I said passionately, 'Priyanka, I love you. I don't know what you feel, but over the years I have realized that you are the only one with whom I want to spend my life. I want to grow old holding your hands. And in your arms I want to breathe my last breath!'

The few seconds of silence that followed seemed to last a century as I sweated profusely. Then from the other side, I heard her laugh softly. She replied, 'You are crazy, Jay! And I love you too!'

From the year 2007, Priyanka and I have been in a beautiful relationship. Yet it was predominantly a long-distance one. For almost a decade, we seldom met. However, the power of our love grew and matured, and we became soulmates.

March 2018, New Delhi, 8.00 p.m.

The Demon Breathes Fire

The unsettling messages from Shalini shook me to the core! In my eyes, the despair in her words clearly implied that this was a life-and-death situation. For two hours, I remained baffled by the momentousness of the case. Despite all atrocities, fate was, once again, sending me on a crusade.

I messaged her back, 'Shalini, please don't do anything drastic. Please give me your phone number. I want to talk to you and understand everything. I know, I can help you.'

Standing alone on the rooftop, I opened my Facebook account on my phone. Shalini had sent me her phone number. With a mind full of apprehension, I dialled the number and waited for a response. As I stood atop the multi-storey building, the dark marquee of the sky stretched overhead, embedded with billions of twinkling stars. At a distance, the ever-bustling alleys of Chandni Chowk were visibly alive with the unending activities of people.

As the call connected, I spoke in haste, 'Hi, Shalini! Is that you? This is Jay here. Jay Alani.'

The voice on the other end was sweet, but panicky. I could sense her angst as she responded, 'Hello Jay. Thank you so much for calling! I am...'

She broke into tears before she could complete the sentence. I calmed her down and asked her, 'Shalini, I will listen to everything. So please calm down and tell me.'

Perhaps the assurance in my voice soothed her. She took a few moments and then related her tale. It was one of pain, sorrow, horror and despondency. As I listened to her story, a maddening storm brewed in my heart...

She started, 'Hi Jay. I am Shalini and I live in Yamuna Nagar along with my parents. The exasperating ordeal began in my otherwise ordinary life about eight months ago. I cannot remember exactly when it all started, but the ghastly episodes came into my life and overwhelmed me. I had never seen a paranormal entity before, but what I see can only be called a demon!

'Yes, it might sound weird and unbelievable, but everything I am saying is true! For the last eight months, I have been visited by the apparition of a legless lady. Her image is always hazy, but I can see her clearly. She is naked, doesn't have legs, and floats around unobstructed covering every nook and corner. I cannot see her face very distinctly, but whatever I can perceive can only be described as gruesome. Her unkempt white hair, her shadowy aura and her fluid frame severely traumatize me. At first, she visited me in the darkness of the night, when I was alone. I screamed in fear a few times, as

I sat and cried all on my own inside my room! I tried to sleep with the lights on, but nothing helped. Soon she started to appear more frequently and even in broad daylight! I was appalled by this frightening experience. As a month passed, I felt caged inside my own body. In the meantime, the apparition began to appear almost everywhere. She swam through the air like an omen, and she started following me like a shadow. Wherever I looked, I could see her staring at me with wrath! Even when I ate, slept, bathed, I could see her. Then, in the next two months, she started to haunt me even in public places. In cinema halls, in shopping malls, in parties and social gatherings, her presence became perpetual. Hidden in the multitude, she fixed her wild stare on me. Oh…I cannot overcome that trauma! Even now as I am talking, she is here! Yes, she is here!'

Shalini paused for a few moments. I could clearly hear her panting. I silently waited for her to resume her story. Then she continued, 'One day, as I was returning from college, I saw her in the bus. She sat right across from me, in an empty seat, and watched me with her all-consuming eyes. I felt a deadly jolt at this that pushed me to the point of insanity. I couldn't scream or cry. I just sat there!'

'She never spoke a word,' Shalini added, 'until about a week later. It was a Sunday. I had just finished taking a shower and was standing in front of the bathroom mirror when she appeared right behind me! She had a sinister smile on her horrific face. I shuddered and turned around. Alas, there was nobody there. My whole body trembled as I stood inside the bathroom. A vapoury mist filled the entire place and a mysterious haze surrounded me. I sat down on the floor with a thud as tears gushed out of my eyes. Then I heard her whisper. Yes, it was a clear feminine voice.

The blood-curdling murmur echoed in my ears: "Shalini, to seek freedom you must obey me! To put an end to our trysts, you have to do what I command you to do. You must KILL YOURSELF or YOUR PARENTS! The old 'Kashmiri Dagger' belonging to your ancestors—the one that is safely kept inside the cupboard—is your weapon. If you don't obey me, I shall kill your parents myself and take you to HELL. The demon within me must be appeased to break the curse and restore order."'

Shalini paused again. I understood that she was experiencing extreme trauma. Then, a while later, she resumed, 'I screamed in great shock. I couldn't figure out the motive behind such a verdict. Yet the voice ceased to speak. I cried for almost an hour. Later that night, I thought that maybe it was my own imagination and I consoled myself. However, the ordeal had just commenced. Since then, every day, I hear those same whispers as many as seven times. I have become a recluse. I cannot tell anyone about my experiences. I fear that I would be marked as a lunatic! Why should I kill myself or my parents? What is this curse? Why is this happening to me? Jay…I cannot kill my parents, so the only option left is for me to to end my own life with that wretched Kashmiri dagger and gain some reprieve. I cannot bear this anymore.'

I interrupted Shalini and asked, 'Shalini, have you spoken with your parents or any friend about this?'

In response, I heard her sobbing. She controlled herself and replied, 'Yes, I did tell my parents. However, when I discussed the matter, they were scared that I was possessed by something evil. They sent me to Brahmanand Ashram for treatment. But that led to a more shameful and miserable episode of my life!'

I steeled myself as I got a hint of what would follow. I remained patient while Shalini continued, 'The baba and his disciples were just perverts who were doing twisted things in the name of God! They treated me like an object of desire whom they could manipulate with their rubbish. I was made to stand naked in the damp living quarters of the dingy ashram in the dead of the night. Jay, they trampled over my modesty as they ogled my body while I stood there helplessly. They even conducted gruesome rituals during which they placed bizarre things on my private parts. The men subjected me to intense psychological torture with their gibberish. Then one day, when I was alone in my room, the baba came in and sat beside me. He touched me and said that the apparition resides within my soul and it needed to be cleansed through sexual intercourse. He smirked and said that only his sperm could purify me and free me from the hauntings. That made me hysterical. I couldn't agree to what he was proposing, and I refused to consent. It was impossible for me to accept it.'

I realized that Shalini was a victim not only of a harrowing haunting, but also of a heinous nexus of criminals! In the name of God and religion, such villains use this common hoax to molest innocent women. My heart started pounding with remorse.

She added, 'The next morning, I fled. I came back home and told my parents that I was absolutely fine and the visit to the ashram had healed me completely. I was scared, very scared. I didn't want to return to that den of iniquity. I only lied to my parents to avoid a disgrace that I wouldn't be able to withstand. Hence, for the last five months, I have been in a state of complete dejection. The ghastly spirit torments me every day; she is omnipresent. She tells me that I don't have much time left. I am shattered—completely!'

As she finished, I felt exhausted too. It had been almost two hours. I sighed and said in a determined voice, 'Shalini, I am there for you! Trust me. Now tell me, how do you want me to help you?'

Her reply struck me like a bolt of thunder. She said, 'No Jay, I don't want your help. I needed to speak to somebody and tell my story. I needed somebody who would believe me. I have made my decision. I shall end my life with the Kashmiri dagger, and put an end to the curse along with my own ordeal. I am happy that when I am gone, at least you will be there to tell the world that I was not a coward who committed suicide! You will be there to tell the world that whatever I did was to save my parents.'

February 2018: Flashback

A Murder of Dreams

The past six months had witnessed my own journey through hell. I had to face the toughest events which brought the edifice of my dreams and love crashing down like a house of cards! As I sat inside my rented apartment in Delhi, I wondered how my entire world turned upside down. Yes, Delhi, I was in Delhi. I was not in Mumbai anymore.

The tale of how I arrived in the city—it brought forth gushes of pain in my festering wounds.

In October 2017, I met Priyanka at Mumbai Airport. She was returning to Patna before her fourth-year MBBS examinations, and her transit was via Mumbai. Despite my uncertain future and my pitiable condition as a struggler, I gathered all the positivity in my soul and met her outside the airport terminal. We were meeting after years and my heart leapt inside my ribcage.

'Could you speak with your family about our future together? We must tell them about us and our wish to get married.' This was what I wanted to say to her. However, standing in front of her, I failed to utter even a single word. My professional instability and the many insecurities that abounded in my life prevented me from speaking, and held me back. We met briefly and soon, she left.

The following month, Priyanka called me and said in a sombre voice, 'Baba and Maa are strictly against our relationship and our future together! Despite your family background, there is one seething question that we cannot ignore—what is your future? Jay, what are you doing with your career?'

Her words were like poison arrows. 'Jay, what professional background are you creating for yourself? You are confused. You don't know where your life is headed. Are you in the creative industry? No. What is your future as a paranormal investigator? Jay, I don't have an answer to any of their questions!'

Despite the truth of her words, I felt insulted and angry. In a fit of rage, I replied, 'That's it. I think the time has come for us to say goodbye to each other! Let us end this painful relationship. I guess we both are correct. Yet I cannot do anything.'

It was just the beginning of a psychological battle. Sitting in my Mumbai apartment, I disconnected the call, blocked her number and deleted all her photos and messages. I did everything to remove my memories of her.

That night, my landlord arrived to collect the pending rent. He abused me like an animal and hurled slurs to my face. I begged like a vagabond in front of him to save myself. Throughout the night, I cried loudly as I reclined on the floor. Perhaps it was the zenith of suffering that my body and soul could take! In that state of sheer distress, I didn't know when the shroud of sleep fell over me and took me away into the world of oblivion.

When I woke up the next morning, my tears had frozen within my heart. I told myself, 'I must leave Mumbai. I must go back! In a world where reality becomes deception at the hands of media tycoons, and truth is just a commodity in the circus of fake entertainment, I didn't see any hope for my own survival. Nobody wants to know about paranormal reality. There is no one in the world who can capture a paranormal entity with the help of gadgets! I just cannot create cheap entertainment in the name of the work that I honestly want to do! My mission is to eliminate blind faith. I'd rather uphold my ideology than be a cool dude. Alas, that is an impossibility!'

I reached Patna a complete failure. I locked myself inside my room and cried for an entire day. Then, the next morning, I went down and faced Baba. I said to him, 'Baba, perhaps you were right and I was wrong. It is impossible for me to survive in Mumbai and pursue my dream. My dream itself is flawed. Thus, I have extinguished that dream within my heart. I don't want to be a paranormal investigator. I just want to lead a normal life.'

Tears came out of my eyes as I spoke, 'Baba, I want to be happy. Please help me...'

Baba hugged me like a child and kissed my forehead. After many years, I was embracing him like a baby. With his help, I paid my dues to my landlord in Mumbai. I stayed in Patna for a few more days. I needed somebody beside me. I was shattered on the inside and was afraid of staying alone. Baba and Maa gave me shelter. Deep inside, I abhorred the career path and my dream of making it big in the area of paranormal investigation. I no longer wanted to pursue something that my countrymen didn't even approve of!

In my despair, I started looking for a solution. I needed a stable career with a decent and respectable income. After much deliberation, I told Baba, 'I will go to Delhi. It is a city where I had attended college. I am acquainted with the city and I have friends there. With their help, I can seek a proper job!'

My dream had crafted the 'angel' within me. The same dream chiselled out the 'demon'.

Thus, I arrived in Delhi and in the first two months of 2018, I managed to land a decent job at a startup. I was a media manager, and my life took a new turn. Destiny gave me a second chance to revive my relationship with Priyanka. Life seemed beautiful once again. With a good job and a handsome salary, my future with Priyanka seemed secure again.

Everything was moving as smoothly as silk; at least I wanted myself to believe that, until the day *the message arrived.*

March 2018, New Delhi, 10.00 a.m.

Meeting Shalini

I understood that the case was not as simple as it seemed. I had an intuition that the apparently straightforward case of paranormal haunting actually had many layers that needed to be unearthed and explored. I sensed that hidden within whatever Shalini had just told me was something much more sinister. I had to act fast.

The next morning, I called up Shalini and said in a convincing voice, 'I need to meet you urgently. Can we catch up tomorrow? I would also like to meet your parents. I need to figure out a method to fight such powerful force.'

Shalini agreed. However, she rejected the idea of me meeting her parents. She asked me to meet her at a café that was next to her college. Thus, the next morning, I headed towards Yamuna Nagar. I waited with bated breath and reached Elegance Café at noon sharp.

Shalini arrived 15 minutes later. There was a subtle beauty in her deep eyes that reflected her innocence. But her harrowing experience of the haunting had left her in a pitiable condition. Though she outwardly looked calm, I could sense a restlessness within her.

We sat down at a table in a relatively secluded corner. I started the conversation on a light-hearted note and then asked, 'Shalini, as we sit here, is the apparition present around us? Can you see her?'

Shalini cast a careful glance and replied in a low voice, 'No. But I am sure she will find me soon.'

'Tell me something, does her face or voice resemble anybody else's?' I asked.

Shalini thought for some time and replied, 'I could never see her face distinctly. Neither did her voice ever sound familiar. But...'

Shalini paused for a while and said something very mysterious, 'At times I feel that I myself am the demon.'

In a choked voice, she said, 'Last night, when I went to bed,

I fell asleep quite soon. A few hours past midnight, I woke up abruptly and saw her. She was floating right above me, near the ceiling. She was laughing mercilessly and pointing her fingers at me. My blood froze within my veins. Then she came close to my face and almost touched my skin. I closed my eyes in shock and opened them after a few seconds. To my absolute surprise, she was gone…'

'Then what happened?' I asked, because I knew that something was missing.

'I felt something hard and cold on my palm,' she replied. 'I looked at it and saw that it was the Kashmiri dagger!'

I sighed and sat back. Then, for the next two hours, I asked her several questions, to which she replied in great detail. I could pinpoint two important facts in Shalini's tumultuous narrative. First, she was very desolate. Second, the answer to her harrowing haunting was hidden somewhere within her.

Then I said, 'Shalini, I need your help. I want to get to the bottom of this mystery. I want to fathom the depth of the demonic powers that this paranormal entity possesses. More importantly, I want to understand why it has chosen you. Promise me that you won't yield to its provocations and cooperate with me. I will call you and talk to you every day. You just need to talk to me and do a few minor things that I ask you to do.'

Maybe the honesty in my words touched her heart and she agreed. Thus began our rendezvous—I called her daily and talked to her for hours. Very slowly, she started to open up. Our conversations lasted for hours and I could feel that Shalini was gradually overcoming her suicidal thoughts. I was able to implant the power to fight in her.

Once she said, 'The apparition still comes and floats around me. Yet my fear has started to metamorphose into strength. Last night, I screamed at her for the first time. I told her I would not be defeated.'

'What did it say to you?' I asked anxiously.

'Her powers are still very strong. She howled at me. Yet I looked into her eyes with all my might. Perhaps destiny wants me to live a bit longer…for somebody,' she said.

I got an inkling that during the course of our talks, Shalini might have fallen in love with me! It was a scary moment for me, but I knew it would be a temporary phase.

A month later, Shalini had to go out of Yamuna Nagar for her examinations. It was the precise moment that I was waiting for. I knew that I had to take that opportunity to meet her parents and visit her home.

April 2018, Yamunanagar

The Zenith

I met Shalini before she went away. I drove from Delhi to Yamuna Nagar and I picked her up from college. As I parked the car, Shalini hugged me like a child and cried. Then she began to speak. Her words opened the last hidden door of the mystery and I was on the brink of a breakthrough.

Shalini said, 'I always knew that the Kashmiri dagger was cursed. Ever since I was a child, I knew it clearly. Now the floating apparition and her verdict has confirmed that notion.'

'Why do you say so?' I asked.

She replied, 'Jay, there is one story that I have never told anybody. I have always been too ashamed and distressed to do so. Yet today, I must tell you everything. When I was about five years old, my cousin uncle used to visit us. He was very good to me in front of Baba and Maa. However, whenever he found me alone, he molested me.'

I was absolutely amazed, so I kept quiet and listened as she continued, 'I was too young to understand what was happening, but I felt very uncomfortable. I used to try and stop him. However, he used to threaten me that he would kill Baba and Maa with the Kashmiri dagger if I ever told anyone anything. In my helplessness, I remained a silent victim of his lust...'

Shalini wept profusely and I consoled her. 'You are a strong girl. What happened was unfortunate. However, it was not your fault and you must never be ashamed of it.'

Shalini replied, 'Now the ghastly woman, in her vapour-like form, keeps referring to that Kashmiri dagger! It is so evil. I abhor it!'

The emotional conversation continued for an hour, but I felt content. I knew I had found my answer and knew my way forward.

In the next five days, when Shalini was away, I met her parents. Unlike my initial perception, her father was very receptive and understood what I said. I gave them some instructions and went back to Delhi.

Then when Shalini returned, I called her up three days later. I spoke to her in a solemn voice and said, 'Listen to me very carefully. Over the past week, I have figured out a solution. It's a battle and I want you to fight.'

Shalini listened to me while I added, 'Tomorrow, at dawn, take the Kashmiri dagger, dip its tip in vermilion and take it with you. Get out of your house and go to the blacksmith's workshop near your college. Give the owner a few bucks to let you in. Then with all your strength, throw the cursed dagger into the furnace! Wait there until it melts completely! Come home and then call me. Can you do this?'

Shalini replied, 'Yes.'

The next day, I felt a strange anxiety. From morning to evening, I couldn't focus on anything. I didn't eat or drink. Finally, at 10.00 p.m., I got the call from Shalini.

As my heart beat wildly, Shalini's radiant voice echoed with vigour. 'Jay! You are my hero! My horrible ordeal is finally over. I did everything you asked me to do and took the Kashmiri dagger with me. The floating ghost followed me like a wolf on the prowl. Then, as I stood in front of the glowing furnace, she tried to burn me down with her furious glare! Yet, with all my might, I threw the dagger into the fire. To my sheer ecstasy, I witnessed the Kashmiri dagger and the horrible phantom get burnt together.'

I experienced a sense of peace in my heart. I asked her, 'Then what happened?'

Shalini replied, 'Then, as I returned home, Baba and Maa called me and asked me to sit down. For the first time in my life, Baba asked me what was troubling me. For the first time in my life, I sensed that he was worried about me. I told them everything and they hugged me. They told me that they would always be my support. Jay, I am so happy. I feel alive again!'

Six Months Later...

The case ended on a positive note. I even told Shalini about Priyanka and me. Gradually, her romantic sentiments matured into a beautiful friendship with the two of us. She now lives a happy and normal life, and is also a successful dentist.

Shalini was not a victim of a haunting. The mysterious door that I had unlocked gave me the answer that I was looking for. I still shiver with fear thinking about her state. I wonder what would have happened had I not been able to intervene properly! Shalini was a victim of something much more dangerous. She was a victim of pareidolia and paracosm.

It was a mental disorder that originated from the trauma that she experienced when she was five years old. The loss of self-respect, the extreme anxiety, and her anger towards her parents for not understanding her pain—all of it triggered Shalini's mental disorder.

Alas, though pareidolia and paracosm set in at a very young age, they actually manifest themselves decades later, when the person has become an adult. Across the world, there have been many instances of pareidolia and paracosm troubling the minds of innocent victims. As I delved deeper, I could recall famous cases of 'shadow persons' and 'invisible friends' that many people have experienced. A shadow person is a typical case of pareidolia, wherein the victim sees human figures in shadows and darkness. Thus, their subconscious minds visualize a paranormal entity within the emptiness. It is a painful state of the mind and can even leave a helpless person in a state of paralysis. Similarly, many young children and even adults, sometimes seem to talk to themselves. Their minds unknowingly visualize the existence of a friend with whom they can communicate. However, in reality, no such friend exists and these people don't have anyone to talk to.

As I sat in my couch, I kept wondering about a recent case that dominated newspaper headlines: the Burari Case. '*The Burari hangings! What a horrific case! The primary suspect Lalit Bhatia was perhaps a victim of paracosm and pareidolia. Because of his deep love for his deceased father, the man's subconscious mind perceived his presence in the house. The dead father directed his son to bring him back from the underworld to meet his beloved family. Such was the power of his hallucinations that Lalit could convince ten family members, including his wife and children, to hang themselves. The mass suicide was a shocking thing that rocked the nation.'*

The uncomfortable feeling lingered in my mind. '*Possibly there are many hidden chapters in that case. Yet I wonder what was going on inside the minds of the innocent victims who chose such a ghastly way to die. The diaries recovered from the investigation reveal that Lalit believed that his father's spirit communicated with him. He believed that performing the deadly ritual would bring back his father's spirit, who, in turn, would rescue them at the right moment and save their lives. Oh, what a colossal loss of human lives! I firmly believe that this is one of the most unfortunate cases of pareidolia and paracosm. Perhaps a timely intervention could have saved the 11 innocent human lives. Maybe they would be alive if I could save them.*'

I shuddered at the thought of what could have happened to Shalini if I did not rescue her at the right time. However, as I unravelled each knot in the mysterious case, deep within my heart, I understood that destiny wanted me to pursue my mission.

The same happened for Shalini. The heinous sexual and psychological abuse that she was subjected to led her to create the image of a demon—the ghastly woman. Her subconscious mind wanted to kill her in order to end her suffering. Moreover, in her heart of hearts, she held her parents guilty for not understanding what she was going through inside their own home! The threats she received from her molester, and the Kashmiri dagger with which he intimidated her, combined to form the subconscious tale of the curse. Shalini's desire for vengeance projected illusions of paranormal hauntings. Yes, pareidolia, coupled with paracosm, created that hoax which tormented her.

This was the mystery that I needed to solve and I felt happy that I had succeeded in doing so.

I knew that to cure the disease, she had to be a warrior. To extinguish the volcano, her subconscious mind needed to banish the evil that haunted her. As Shalini threw the Kashmiri dagger into the flames, the fire burnt away her fears, along with the paranormal entity haunting. Then she received additional support from her parents, whom I had already told everything. My instinct guided me to successfully solve this complex psychological puzzle! Often, such hauntings need a logical and human approach, rather than hi-tech gadgets. The root cause of the problem needed to be eliminated and I felt relieved that I could do so for Shalini. As the horrendous memories of her past sufferings and the fears associated with the Kashmiri dagger were addressed and eliminated, her soul was purged of all her fears. The demon was defeated by the purity and strength within her heart.

As I sat inside my room and looked out the open window, I sighed. '*Yes, we are our own "angel" and our own "demon". Today, as I see Shalini rise from the ashes like a phoenix, I feel that my mission in life is still going strong. Paranormal reality is an inherent part of my own existence. I am...the Paranormal Boy!*'

5

Kill Me Please

'Whatever doesn't kill you makes you stronger.'

One Summer Night in 1985, 'Mem ki Kabr', Dagshai Cemetery

The 'Mother' Watches: A Tale from Folklore

Manohar Singh was a visitor from the plains. He had come to the nearby village of Chunawad for work. But he had also heard the fable of Mem ki Kabr.

It was a common rumour: *'If you break off a piece of the Englishwoman's tomb and let a pregnant woman keep it, she will surely give birth to a boy!'*

Manohar and his wife were expecting their first child in a few months, and the needles of greed pricked at his heart. Being illiterate, he asked, 'But how do you know which grave it is?'

The rumours had whispered the answer to him: 'It's the tomb with the carving of a lady reclining with a child in her arms, and an angel watching over them. Easy to find…'

So one night later, Manohar slipped into Dagshai Cemetery.

The half-moon poured down its silken light, trying to wash away the dense shroud of darkness. The uneven terrain of the ancient graveyard was dotted with the old graves of British men and women, under the shadow of tall trees. Though the cemetery stood in the plain ground of a valley, the land was deceptively uneven.

Past midnight, Manohar crept over a secluded stretch of the boundary wall. His pupils widened to drink in the darkness surrounding him, though in places, the night seemed to have frozen into solid blocks of blackness. Alone, he walked ahead anxiously, not wanting anyone to find out about his mission. His eyes scoured the grounds for Mem ki Kabr. A faint mist clung to the ground, and the air was a little cold because of the altitude.

He passed a few graves, crossed a cluster of ferns, and then halted abruptly. Something loomed ahead of him. His eyes lit up with excitement.

'Yes! I've found it!'

The fabled grave stood before him. A strangely dense mass of mist hung around it, and as soon as he approached, the fog thinned and a pale halo glowed around the tombstone. Manohar took out a small chisel and a hammer, and stepped forward.

Just then, the silence shattered—pierced by an unnerving chorus of screams! Terrified, he froze. But then he chuckled nervously. 'Wretched red foxes, wild frogs, and owls singing in harmony—making such ghostly music!'

Steeling himself, he reached the base of the tombstone. From there, the entire grave was visible. The marble was exquisitely carved—a mother cradling her infant in her arms, an angel blessing them from above. Yet vandals had scarred the work, chipping away at its beauty—others like him, who had stolen pieces of the tomb before.

On the side, the inscription read: *'To the sacred and loving memory of my wife, Mary Rebecca Weston, who died at Dagshai, 10th December 1909, and our unborn Babe.'* But Manohar, being illiterate, could not understand it.

He touched the corner of the grave, right where the infant had been carved, and raised his hammer to strike. But his hands froze.

'EEEEEeeeeeee!' An icy scream tore through the stillness.

This was no animal's cry. It was the voice of a woman.

In horror, the hammer and chisel slipped from his hands. Manohar stumbled backward, tripped, and rolled down the slope. As he scrambled to his feet, he saw it…

A woman stood on top of Mem ki Kabr. Her form was hideous, her clothes torn, her mouth twisted in a devilish scream. She was real. Manohar knew he was not hallucinating. For a heartbeat, he thought the apparition would leap at him and rip open his chest.

Trembling, he begged, 'No! Forgive me… I won't touch it! Please don't kill me!'

The ghastly figure stood atop the tombstone and howled like a wolf. Manohar, with what little courage still remained with him, turned around and ran. He madly sprinted through the graveyard, stumbling over rocks, scraping his limbs on the ground—but he didn't stop. At last, with his final ounce of strength, he vaulted over the wall, staggered into a nearby settlement, and pounded on the door of a house, before collapsing and falling unconscious.

For five days, Manohar lay traumatized. When he finally recovered, the villagers warned him: 'No one from our villages goes near that cemetery. It is haunted. The ghost of Mary Rebecca Weston roams that ground, guarding her unborn child.'

Manohar remembered his dreadful encounter, screamed in terror, and fainted again…

Flashback: 1908–09, Army Cantonment, Dagshai Town, Himachal Pradesh

The History behind the Legend

Major George Weston of the Royal Army Medical Corps was posted in the small cantonment town of Dagshai, Himachal Pradesh. Originally known as Daagh-e-Shahi during the Mughal era, Dagshai was once a secluded corner of the Himalayas where convicts were deported.

Situated at an altitude of 5,689 feet, the cantonment was founded in 1847 by the East India Company, which secured five villages from Maharaja Bhupinder Singh of Patiala. These villages were Dabbi, Badhtiala, Chunawad, Jawag and Dagshai.

Major Weston was a benevolent doctor who dedicated his life to his duty. He lived in Dagshai with his beloved wife Mary Rebecca Weston. The couple was happily married, and Mary often assisted her husband in his work. Yet, despite 17 years of marriage, they remained childless. That was their only sorrow, which cast a shadow on their otherwise happy lives.

Then, one day, a sadhu baba arrived in the village. A chance meeting brought him face to face with Major Weston and Mary. The sadhu baba touched Mary's hands, closed his eyes, and said softly, 'I can sense a colossal pain in your hearts—the pain that even overshadows your love. Only a child can fill that emptiness.'

He turned to the couple and asked, 'Sahib, if I give your wife an amulet, will you have faith in it?'

Major Weston looked into Mary's eyes, then nodded. The sadhu baba took out an amulet and said, 'Madam, wear this on your right arm. Soon the gods will bless you with a child.'

The next morning, the sadhu baba left, but Major Weston and Mary placed their faith in his amulet. In their desperation, an unexplained feeling of trust took hold of their hearts. And indeed, as if by divine grace, Mary conceived after a few months.

Major Weston was ecstatic. Holding his wife close, he whispered, 'My love, after 17 years, our dream will finally come true.'

But not all dreams materialize into happiness. Some dreams wither into nightmares. On 10 December 1909, eight months into her pregnancy, Mary died during labour, along with her unborn child.

Major Weston was shattered. His world collapsed in a single night—not only had he lost his beloved wife, but he had also forfeited the child who had not even seen the first light of day.

In her loving memory, Major Weston commissioned a beautiful tombstone. Upon it, he engraved the following inscription expressing his grief:

'To the sacred and loving memory of my wife, Mary Rebecca Weston, who died at Dagshai, 10th December 1909, and our unborn Babe.'

It is said that Major Weston returned to England after that tragedy and never remarried.

Mid-August 2018, Varanasi, Riverbank Opposite Manikarnika Ghat

A Sacrifice

I sat inside the dingy shack, pondering what I had just experienced.

I had arrived in Varanasi two days earlier, and met the two boatmen Nishant and Sashi. Amidst the bustling, overcrowded streets, my real-estate agent Vinay had led me through a narrow, secluded lane where he introduced me to them. Almost immediately, Vinay melted into the crowd, leaving me alone with the two men.

They assured me together, 'Every word you've heard about the ritual is true! Sahib, the great priests of Aghor Tantra possess enormous powers. Your wish will come true.'

'All right,' I had replied. 'What do we do next?'

'The rate is 50,000 bucks, non-negotiable,' said Sashi, the taller of the two.

I nodded in agreement. Nishant leaned closer and added, 'Meet us at the jetty beside the ghat. From there, we'll cross the river to the opposite bank of Manikarnika Ghat. That's where everything will be performed, and we'll introduce you to the right people.'

So this morning, I met Nishant and Sashi again, paid them an advance of 20,000, and purchased items worth another 10,000 for the ritual. By evening, the three of us boarded a small boat and ferried across the river to the deserted bank opposite Manikarnika Ghat.

As we disembarked, I noticed the unsettling emptiness of the place. The air was heavy with silence, and the forested path we walked through seemed to lead deeper into something sinister. At the end of the trail stood a cluster of filthy, crumbling shacks.

'Welcome to the abode of the Aghor Baba,' Sashi muttered.

The sun had already set, and darkness had fallen over the place. I had been waiting inside the shack for nearly half an hour when Nishant finally returned.

'Sahib, don't worry,' he whispered. 'Your contract to kill your enemy will strike him like thunder. It is a flawless method of the tantric kind. Now, please follow me.'

I rose and followed him outside. In the open space between the shacks, Aghor Baba and his men were seated. Their crimson robes glowed eerily in the firelight, their matted grey locks and long beards lent them a dreadful appearance. Their eyes—red and burning—radiated pure ruthlessness.

As I sat before the baba, he spoke in a booming baritone voice, 'Aghor Tantra is the highest level of tantric practice. With our supernatural powers, we can do anything.'

I kept quiet as I listened to his blustering speech.

'Now,' he thundered, 'tell me the name of the enemy you want to kill. Give me a photograph of that person!'

I cast a quick glance around. The preparations for the sacrificial ritual were already underway. Beside the baba lay two human skulls, and there were bones scattered here and there. His disciples chanted, invoking powers they claimed were bestowed by Yama, the God of death, and by Goddess Kali. They moved with a hypnotic rhythm designed to break the strongest of willpowers. The process, they said, demanded that the one commissioning the killing be present in person—body and soul—so the sacrifice could be completed.

I fumbled and said, 'I don't have a picture of my enemy. But I can give you his details—his name, his date of birth…'

Aghor Baba laughed. 'Fine. First, pay the mediators. Then go inside, change into the ritualistic garb, and return when I summon you.'

I nodded. His eyes glowed with menace as he leaned forward. 'Are you ready to eat human flesh from a corpse? Are you ready to complete the ritual? Do you have the courage? Because if you falter, the sacrifice will claim your own life!'

I locked my gaze with his, and answered, 'Yes. I am.'

'Then speak,' he said. 'Tell me the name of your enemy so I can prepare my tantra.'

I inhaled deeply and replied, 'His name is… Jay Alani.'

2 Months Ago

A Strange Plan Takes Shape

In Delhi, I started working at a production house that primarily handled government advertisements. Though hired as a writer, I found myself doing a range of things—script-writing, voice-overs, and more. Immersed in my job, I had virtually given up on my dreams when, one day, something unexpected happened.

The dubbing manager at my office said, 'Jay, you have a nice voice, and I know about your passion for paranormal investigation. You've got so many incredible cases to share with the world. Why don't you try your luck with podcasts? Trust me, it's trending—you must explore this opportunity.'

His advice struck a chord with me, and I began to think about it seriously. Over the next few days, I researched podcasting and dug deeper into the audio space. A new flame ignited in my heart: *Yes, this could be my medium to spread awareness about my work! The industry is still niche, and I can carve out my own space.*

With renewed enthusiasm, I reached out to a few companies. Yet again, my ideas were rejected—the lack of 'commercial masala' in my content failed to entice them. But I didn't lose hope. One evening, I came across an app called HubHopper. Their website looked promising for new podcasters, and I noted down a phone number.

The next morning, I called them. A man named Nikhil answered. After introducing myself and telling him that I wanted to record my case diaries, he replied, 'Your ideas are quite interesting. Can you come down to our office today? We're in Greater Kailash.'

Since I lived in Saket, the office was quite close. 'Yes,' I said, 'I'll be there.'

The office turned out to be warm and welcoming. We had an hour-long meeting where I poured my heart out and told them everything I intended to do—narrating my experiences as a paranormal investigator.

Finally, they said, 'Please record and send us audios. We'll edit and upload them as podcasts. Unfortunately, we won't be able to pay you anything. But we assure you that the reach will be good.'

Honestly, I wasn't in a position to demand money. So I agreed. I knew I could use the recording studio at my office to record the podcasts. Walking out of their office that day, I felt hopeful.

That afternoon I asked my boss, in the presence of the dubbing manager, 'Sir, may I ask for a favour? After working hours, could I use the recording studio to record some personal audios?'

Luck was on my side. I got approval to use the studio until 8.00 p.m. every day. And so began my podcasting journey. Every evening, I recorded my stories and sent them to HubHopper. That's how it all started…

HubHopper uploaded the audios, and slowly, people began listening to my case files. Days passed, then weeks, and after a month or two—it clicked!

My podcast broke records. Listeners began streaming my case diaries in a loop! Nikhil and his team were ecstatic, and one evening I got a call: 'Jay, your podcast is now officially a superhit!'

I couldn't believe my eyes when I saw my phone flooded with messages, my social media followers multiplying by the thousands, and my email inbox overflowing. That's when I realized—I just could not give up on my dreams.

My heart told my mind: *We live in a world overflowing with lies. People are bombarded with fabrications crafted to serve other people's hidden motives. Wherever we look—TV, newspapers, office discussions, and even at home, where couples lie to each other—we find distorted versions of the truth. And slowly, we've begun to accept these lies as life's truths. No, this cannot continue. My podcast must break that taboo. A handful of people cannot decide what kind of content millions in this country deserve to be exposed to. I will tell the truth through my stories.*

Yes, *Paranormal Reality*, Season 1, was a success, but somewhere in that struggle, Jay Alani, the paranormal investigator, got lost in an opaque mist, bereft of a sense of purpose.

Glimpses from my recent past continued to haunt me like the ghost of my own soul. So even after completing

Paranormal Reality, Season 1, I was, once again, completely lost. Despite the popularity, I knew I wasn't making any money. My only source of income was still my job. I needed that job to survive and pursue my plans.

In my frustration, I questioned myself: *'Can I ever quit my job and become a full-time paranormal investigator? No. Why? Why can't I do it? Why can't this country support a good cause?'*

It was a bad monsoon that year, and there were heavy showers. I sat inside my bedroom, on my bed, and wept like a child. Flashes of the abuses my landlord had hurled at me in Mumbai came back to me like burning splinters! My grandmother had always treated me like a king. My Baba had always pampered me like his prince. I belonged to a respectable, somewhat affluent family. And yet, I had faced so much abuse.

'No, I am not a beggar. And I didn't deserve to be abused,' I cried aloud. *'But even today, I cannot prove myself.'*

'What am I doing now?' I asked myself as the thunder growled outside. *'I am still a failure. I cannot do my job properly, and I cannot dream my dream properly either!'*

I writhed in pain, in desperation—until suddenly, my eyes fell on a number saved in my phone. It read: Real Estate Agent—Vinay (Varanasi).

In a flash of lightning, I remembered him. A few days ago, I had met Vinay in Delhi, where he shared his number with me. From him, I had once heard the words: *'Sahib, come to Varanasi once. It is a mystical place. I know you've been to the city quite a few times, but I can show you another side of it—the side where one can draw up a contract to kill, and black magic will do the job!'*

Like a robot, I dialled his number. My heart and my mind were at war. I had succeeded with the podcast, but I still felt like a failure in my mission. In front of my eyes, I saw the death of that dream because I realized no one truly believed in my plans.

As Vinay answered the call, I said in a determined voice, 'Vinay, this is Jay. Remember me?'

'Oh yes, Sir, I do. Please tell me what I can do for you,' he responded in his amicable voice.

'Vinay, I need your help,' I added. 'I want a contract to kill. Yes, I am serious about it.'

A moment of silence followed. Then Vinay said, in a sombre voice, 'Sir, come to Varanasi immediately.'

Mid-August 2018, Varanasi, Riverbank opposite Manikarnika Ghat

The Face-Off

I got up from the ground and went inside the shack once again—guided this time by the two mediators Nishant and Sashi. A quick glance at my watch told me it was 8.00 p.m. There was an overwhelming stench in the air, probably from the toxins consumed by the accomplices of Aghor Baba.

Through the tiny window, I looked across the river. On the opposite bank stood Manikarnika Ghat. In the darkness, a few points of light burnt boldly. They were the flames of the pyres where the dead were being cremated. It is said the fires at Manikarnika never go out, and that those who are cremated there achieve liberation from their sins, and their path to the underworld is made pure. Yet, despite its auspiciousness, the sight stirred a strange melancholy feeling in me. Why was I sad? Why did tears gather in my eyes? I didn't know.

Inside the shack, I could hear the sound outside grow louder. A grand arrangement was underway. My thoughts spiralled: *Why am I here tonight? Why did I choose to be a paranormal investigator? What am I trying to prove by coming to this strange place?*

A cool breeze from the river slipped in through the window. I breathed it in and told myself: '*If you want to love who you are, you cannot hate the experiences that shaped you. Am I doing that? What has my mission been? What am I proving tonight?*'

'Sahib, come. It is time,' Nishant's voice interrupted my trance.

'You must prepare now,' Sashi added.

'You need to be naked for this ritual,' Nishant explained. 'Only you can perform it, and it must be done correctly.'

I pushed aside all inhibitions, stripped down to my underwear, and stood there. They handed me two earthen vials: one with an oil that reeked with a strange odour, and the other with *vibhuti*—ashes from the cremation grounds.

'Smear these all over your body,' Sashi commanded.

'And don't forget to carry the ₹20,000. You must give it to Aghor Baba directly,' Nishant added.

Spellbound, I obeyed. Then I stepped out into the open. At the centre of the camp sat Aghor Baba in front of a sacrificial fire. Its devilish glow lit up his equally devilish face. He was visibly drunk—so were all his accomplices. Every one of them was naked. The sight was crude and grotesque.

I sat down opposite him, the fire blazing between us. Two skulls were placed in my hands. The chants began. Someone handed me a piece of sweetmeat, urging me to eat it quickly. I hesitated, then put it inside my mouth.

Almost at once, the barbaric drama began. Whatever they had laced that sweet with caused hallucinations. Fear gripped me—it was terrifying.

At the peak of the ritual, Aghor Baba ordered me to circle the fire and pour alcohol into the flames from the skulls. My vision spun; nausea rose until I thought I would collapse. As I stared into the fire, blurred and reeling, I saw a face in the flames.

It was my Maa.

In that instant, I realized: life might be difficult, but it is precious. It is beautiful.

At last, the ritual ended. One of the men doused me with a bucket of water. I gasped, wiping it from my face, and as if by magic, I was no longer intoxicated.

Aghor Baba looked at me with a sinister smile. 'The ritual is complete. Go, take a holy dip in the river, then dress yourself. Leave now. In three days, your enemy will die! Hahaha!'

I said nothing. I went straight to the river, took a dip in its waters, got dressed, and returned with the two boatmen.

As the boat rocked across the river, I whispered to myself: *Finally, I have killed the Jay Alani who doubted my own mission. At last, Jay Alani, the paranormal investigator, is free from all evils. Thank you, Maa, for opening my eyes.*

The next day, I returned to Delhi. One by one, seven days passed—but I didn't die. I am still alive. Aghor Baba's black magic could not kill me.

And as I left Varanasi, I thought: *what if such rituals really had the power to kill? What would the world become then?*

That night, I understood the limits to which people can stoop to satisfy their most disgusting motives.

And I told myself: *Yes, my mission is necessary. Blind faith must be eradicated from the world. And I must remain the torch-bearer of this mission.*

10 October 2018, Dagshai Cemetery, 6.00 p.m.

The Exploration Begins

Sometime between Seasons 1 and 2 of *Paranormal Reality*, I received information about Dagshai Cemetery and the haunted 'Mem ki Kabr'.

Intrigued, I decided to investigate. My research revealed the tragic tale of Mary Rebecca Weston and how the repeated vandalism of her grave had left it desecrated.

Ten days later, I was in Dagshai.

The old cantonment town in Himachal Pradesh's Solan district still retained its alpine charm. About 11 kilometres off the main highway, it seemed caught in a time warp. I checked into a modest motel, prepared for the October chill with warm clothes.

Before evening, I prepared for the exploration. Any investigation in such an environment demanded planning and equipment. I carried a high-powered flashlight, a sturdy walking stick that could also serve as a weapon, insect repellents and medicines, and supplies to build a bonfire—I intended to spend the night in the wilderness. I even secured written permission from the village head. Hydrated and well fed, I set out.

As the sun sank and the veil of evening descended, I

reached the cemetery. To my surprise, the place was both secluded and unguarded, despite lying close to a populated village.

I walked in. The alpine beauty of the surroundings only enhanced the general eeriness of the cemetery. The ground was uneven, dotted with the ancient graves of British men and women. Their weathered tombstones stood like fragile sentinels, quietly telling the stories of souls buried beneath the cold soil. The wind that swept through made strange sounds—like whispers from the departed spirits who, perhaps, longed to speak to me—a rare visitor in their lonely resting place.

But my eyes searched for something else. *Where is the grave of Mary Rebecca Weston?*

It was a full moon night. By 6.00 p.m., darkness had already enveloped everything; the crimson twilight had slipped away unnoticed. The nocturnal world stirred around me. Insects and unseen creatures filled the air with their shrieks and calls—strange sounds that might terrify someone unfamiliar with the wilderness. But my explorations as a paranormal investigator had taught me not to flinch.

Then I noticed it—a cage. From a distance it looked like an enclosure, but as I approached, I saw it clearly: thick steel wire mesh that was put up around a single grave. I raised my flashlight. Inside lay Mary's grave.

The once-vandalized tomb had been restored to its original glory, now shielded from further harm by the wire mesh. The marble monument glimmered in the pale light—beautifully carved with the figure of a mother holding her infant, watched over by an angel.

On the side, I read the inscription:

'To the sacred and loving memory of my wife Mary Rebecca

Weston who died at Dagshai, 10th December 1909, and our unborn Babe.'

A wave of calm—and melancholy—swept over me. A few paces away stood a large tree. I went under it and lit a bonfire.

10 October 2018, Dagshai Cemetery, 11.15 p.m.

The Endless Wait

The chill in the air grew sharper, and I huddled closer to the fire. I knew I had a long vigil ahead. *I won't leave before dawn,* I told myself.

From my bag, I pulled out a packet of potato chips and began munching slowly. A glance at my wristwatch told me it wasn't midnight yet. The village beyond the cemetery was drowned in slumber, while I sat alone inside among the ancient graves, waiting for…something. What exactly, I wasn't sure.

Minutes crawled by. My own heartbeat grew loud in my ears. And then—it happened.

Piercing the silence came the unmistakable sound of footsteps crunching over dry foliage. Yes, footsteps. Clear, deliberate steps—so it could not be a wild animal. A cold shiver ran down my spine as I realized that it was a human being.

Something—or someone—was rushing towards me. My heart pounded in my chest. I gripped the stick tightly in my right hand, the flashlight in my left. I kept it unlit as I waited. The sound came from behind me, closing in fast, as though the thing was about to pounce.

The footsteps sounded furious. Whatever it was, anger informed its very rhythm. Even so, I tried to stay calm. I would not turn around until the last moment. I wanted it close to me. I wanted to confront it—even if it was not of this world.

The wind rose suddenly, howling through the cemetery. The footsteps stopped right behind me—so close that I could almost feel something pressing against my skin. With a surge of energy, I spun around and switched on the flashlight.

Whoosh! An icy blast whipped against my face. The space behind me was empty. The footsteps that had been so loud, so real, were gone—snuffed out in an instant.

The cold wind swept over the cemetery, rushing towards Mem ki Kabr. It blew away the mist that had settled thickly over the tomb. The beam of my flashlight followed it. I stared hard at the grave—and saw nothing.

10 October 2018, Dagshai Cemetery, 12.45 a.m.

The 'Mother' Weeps

It was a strange and spooky moment. I gathered my things and moved closer to the grave. My mind was made up. I sat right beside the caged tomb, while the remnants of my bonfire still glowed faintly at a distance.

Whatever it is, I shall wait for its return, I told myself. I will search and find it. I am not here to vandalize the tomb. I believe in the realms of both the living and the dead, and I respect their coexistence. Nothing can harm me.

A glance at my wristwatch revealed that it was almost 1.00 a.m. My nerves were frayed with anticipation, and I experienced no urge of sleep.

My gaze settled on Mary's grave. The restoration work was immaculate. Through the rails of the cage, I could clearly see the mother's carved face. Her marble eyes seemed alive—filled with maternal affection, but also a profound sadness, the desperation of a mother trying to shield her unborn child from the claws of predators. Then I noticed something I hadn't before. A smile. Was it there earlier? Or had it only just surfaced now, in the dead of the night? I stared, wondering, as silence wrapped itself around me.

I turned away for a moment, reaching for my water bottle. That's when the silence was shattered.

'Oooooo... Ooohhh...'

The sound was unearthly. A shrill, heart-rending wail—a woman's cry of mourning. The voice was distinct, close, and unmistakably coming from Mem ki Kabr.

Before I could turn around, something flickered at the edge of my vision. A pale, feminine figure dashed past the cage. Too quick for me to see clearly—but real enough to jolt me to the core.

Strangely, my fears abandoned me. With a sudden spurt of strength, I leapt up and ran. The sound of footsteps crunching over the foliage was sharp and clear. I chased them like a madman.

And then—I stumbled. My foot snagged on the rough ground, my body lurched, and I fell.

I didn't just fall. I was plunged into a pit. An open grave.

I landed with a thud, my head striking the wet soil. Pain flashed through my body. Then—something touched my skin.

A convulsion seized my entire being as the realization sank in.

I was not alone in the grave.

The icy skin of another body brushed against mine, and its cold breath swept across me.

10 October 2018, Dagshai Cemetery, 1.45 a.m.

The Pinnacle of Irony and Grief

Within seconds, I gathered my wits and realized what had just happened. Crouching beneath me was a woman. And she was no apparition. She was very much alive, and shaking with fear and astonishment, while I was left utterly embarrassed.

Quickly, I scrambled out of the grave and pulled her up as well. From her attire, it was clear that she was a local villager. My fear disappeared; anger took its place. I flashed light on her face and demanded, 'What are you doing inside a grave in the middle of the night? Don't lie to me—or I'll call the police. Do you even have permission to be here?'

She grinned, displaying her dirty teeth, and snapped back, 'It's none of your business! Sahib, do *you* have permission to be here at night? Then how can you question me?'

I'd had enough. I lashed out at her, telling her harshly that I was not some vagabond but here for an official exploration with written permission from the village head. I needed to frighten her into revealing her true intentions. Perhaps she thought I was a powerful man who could have her thrown in jail, because finally she broke.

'Sahib, please don't call the police,' she begged. 'I promise I won't do it again. I am a poor woman from the next village. I am only doing the same work my mother once did to earn some money.'

'What work? Tell me everything,' I sternly pressed her.

She was well past middle age, her red sweater and worn saree was filthy from poverty. Clutching a sack, she said, 'On certain nights, I come here alone and chip pieces from the gravestones. I sell them to people who believe in the fable of Mem ki Kabr. Now the grave is caged, but years ago, my mother used to fetch pieces from that tomb itself. Sahib, we are poor villagers. People pay ₹20,000, sometimes ₹50,000, for a piece!'

'Then what about the screams? The footsteps? Were you trying to frighten me?' I snapped.

'No, Sahib,' she stammered in fear. 'Please believe me—I did no such thing. When I saw you near Mem ki Kabr, I got scared you'd catch me. So I hid inside that grave…'

Her story made me ache inside. The sheer depths of blind faith in this country! I marvelled at the way ignorance could drive the poor to such acts of desecration.

'I don't believe you,' I said firmly. 'You are a thief. Under Section 297 of the IPC, tampering with graves can land you in jail. Promise me you'll abandon this shameful line of work.'

She nodded frantically, weeping and pleading for mercy, then fled into the darkness.

I returned to my spot and sat waiting for dawn. An uneasiness gnawed at me, though I couldn't name it. At last, the first crimson rays of dawn washed over the cemetery. I rose with a sigh. 'Oh, what an experience,' I muttered as I slowly made my way towards the gate.

But then I turned back for one last look at Mem ki Kabr, standing in the misty distance. And in that instant, I realized why I was feeling uneasy—and I shuddered.

The voice I had heard earlier, the mournful wail piercing the silence—it did not belong to the woman I later caught. The fleeting figure I had glimpsed was not clothed in red. Which meant that she hadn't lied.

A tentacle of mist coiled over Mary's grave as these questions clouded my mind.

Was there someone else in the cemetery last night? Or had I truly encountered a remnant of some sort of energy—a grieving soul? Was the villager lying to cover her tracks, or did the spirit of Mary Rebecca Weston reveal herself to me?

Had the sorrowful mother wailed to share her pain? Was she the true origin of both the folklore and the legend? I had no answers. Perhaps none will ever be found.

But I believe this much: a thin, invisible veil separates the mortal world from the paranormal one. And while blind faith must be eradicated, the world of spirits is not what greedy conmen claim it is.

The paranormal aura of Mem ki kabr is not born of terror. It is the lingering energy of a mother's love for her child—pure and eternal.

6

The Goddess of Sex

'When "faith" becomes "blind", it dies to become a devil.'

November 2018, New Delhi, 12.23 a.m.

The 'Demon' Spews 'Venom'

Manthan opened his eyes, startled awake from his sleep. He could hear his heart pounding. In the suffocating darkness of the night, he searched for the source of the lustful feminine voice. Yes—it was a voice he knew all too well.

'Open your eyes,' a woman whispered in his ears. 'Look at me! I am here to take you to the heavenly world of desire!'

'No! I don't want to go anywhere with you,' Manthan cried, his entire body slick with sweat.

'You must come,' the razor-sharp voice reiterated. 'You are mine tonight…and every night!'

'Please forgive me! Please!' Manthan wept. He tried to drag himself out of the bed but his body refused to move. A terrifying numbness had overtaken his limbs. Tears streamed down his face as he begged, 'I did everything you asked. I did it shamelessly. Ahhhh… Vaishali hates me and I am ruined. Now, please, spare me!'

'Come—or I shall reveal that little secret of yours!' screamed the feminine voice.

A thick mist flooded the room, and a red aura began to shimmer and spread within the ghostly haze. From its depths emerged the woman. Draped in sensuous fabric and adorned with poisonous flowers dangling from her neck, waist and arms, she glided forward with provocative grace and pressed her lips to Manthan's forehead.

Her kiss was cold as ice, but it burnt like a venomous sting. Manthan shuddered, but his body was paralysed. He tried to scream for help—yet his voice caught in his throat.

The woman stepped back, straightening her spine like a predator poised to strike. The crimson haze thickened, swallowing the entire room until his vision blurred. He could not comprehend what was happening.

Then, without any warning, a thunderous force scattered the mist. As his vision cleared, Manthan saw that the woman had transformed into a massive serpent. The monstrous snake flicked its enormous red tongue, then hurled itself at him.

'Ooohhh God… Please save me! Ahhhh…'

As the predator swooped on its prey and engulfed him completely, the suffocating mist and crimson haze swept back into the room, drowning everything once more.

A Few Days Later

A Strange Phone Call

The episode in Varanasi had left a lasting impact on both my body and my mind. As my podcast gained greater acceptance among the audience, I pushed myself harder to prove my worth beyond all conceivable limits. Like a fanatic, I became consumed by the madness of establishing paranormal reality and eradicating blind faith.

In my strange compulsion to answer every possible question, I mocked myself with my own words: '*You must take risks! Without risk, you cannot uncover the darkness that hides in the deepest chambers of the abyss. Your audience wants to hear you—you must not disappoint them. Go confront the devils! Go fight the monsters! Your entire existence is dedicated to your mission to burn down that black curtain, so your duty becomes* divine! *Yes…take every opportunity!*'

Because of this obsession, I forgot my greater responsibility towards my family. I forgot that I was about to dive headlong into an active volcano that could burn me to ashes. I was entering dangerous, uncharted waters, blind to the fact that this attempt could very well cost me my life. I forgot to do my duty towards Baba, Maa, my family, my love Priyanka, and towards my followers and subscribers. Yet, on the flipside, I am certain that had I not taken those drastic steps and faced those perilous moments, I might never have done justice to my crusade against blind faith. But at that time, I was far too desperate.

Then one winter morning, I got a phone call. The voice on the other end was anxious:

'Hello? Are you Mr Jay Alani?'

As I replied, I could sense the apprehension in his voice, the weight in his heavy breaths. He continued, 'Sir, my name is Arvind Nagpal. I am a 76-year-old retired government officer. Jay, I really need your help to save my grandson…'

Something struck me, and I answered, 'Sir, please, tell me

everything without any hesitation! I promise I will try to help in every way possible.'

'Jay,' Mr Nagpal said in a sombre voice, 'my grandson Manthan is in grave danger. I believe he is...possessed by something devilish. I think he is under a ghastly spell.'

'Sir,' I urged, 'please tell me more. I need every detail.'

'Manthan has been behaving very strangely for the last few days,' he said. 'To be precise—three weeks ago, he went on a week-long college excursion to Madhya Pradesh. A few days after returning, the bouts of abnormal behaviour began. At first, he showed signs of nervousness. Then, day by day, I watched him retreat into an invisible shell. His limbs trembled, and he perspired heavily even while sitting with others. Soon things worsened. He began screaming out loud at midnight, gripped by extreme fear! Last night, I rushed into his room after hearing his cries for help. He was panting for breath, writhing in pain. When I asked what had happened, he said something that left me horrified. Jay... my grandson believes that Kamini, the Goddess of Sex, is going to kill him!'

I exclaimed, 'Goddess of what? I have never heard of such a goddess in my entire life!'

'Jay, please help us,' Mr Nagpal wept. 'Manthan is an unfortunate child. He lost his parents when he was 12 years old. Now, he is the only family I have left, and I cannot sit by and watch him sink into some supernatural abyss.'

'Don't worry, Sir,' I said with determination. 'Please give me your address. I will come meet you.'

As I noted down the address, I told myself: '*I think I know what lies behind this haunting—and I must get to the root of that fear. Only then can I save Manthan. But I don't have much time.*'

Fortunately, the address was close by, and I resolved to visit Mr Nagpal's house the very next morning.

Mid-November 2018, Pitampura, New Delhi

A Helpless Victim of 'Pain'

I parked my car in front of the little bungalow. It was a modest house in a beautiful locality, reflective of its simplicity. The winter morning was still lazily maturing into a new day. It was 9.00 a.m. when I stepped forward and knocked on the door.

Mr Nagpal opened it himself and greeted me. He was a tall, frail man whose face was marked by subtle strength—perhaps the divine strength needed to stay alive long enough to see his grandchild build a decent life for himself. He smiled, ushered me into the living room, and asked me to sit.

He offered me water and coffee, but I was too impatient. I asked, 'Where is Manthan?'

'He is upstairs, in his room,' said Mr Nagpal.

'Sir, please take me to him,' I said. 'Then introduce me as—'

'He knows you're coming,' interrupted Mr Nagpal. 'I told him about you, and surprisingly, he already knows you very well. He follows you on social media and is aware of your work.'

'Good.' I smiled. 'That makes things much easier. Let's go and meet him first.'

As we entered Manthan's room, I sensed something peculiar. The only window was tightly shut, with heavy curtains drawn across it. A single electric bulb hung from a corner and cast a dull glow. The air felt thick with negativity, as though the very walls had a hallucinatory energy that toyed with the human senses.

Manthan, a lanky young boy, sat hunched on the bed, his arms folded over his legs, his head drooping between them. He lifted his face and looked at us. Despite his nervous, withdrawn demeanour, his eyes brightened when he saw me.

I knew what I had to do. I rushed forward, flung open the curtains, and unlatched the window. Immediately, a cool breeze and an abundance of sunlight flooded the room, illuminating every corner with warmth and life.

Then I turned to Mr Nagpal and said firmly, 'I'd like to speak with Manthan in private. Can you please step outside and close the door? I need complete privacy while I spend some time with him. I hope you understand.'

Mr Nagpal nodded and quietly left. I locked the door behind him and sat beside Manthan. Even before I could speak, he began to weep uncontrollably.

I didn't say a word at first—just touched his hands softly. He clung to me like a child and sobbed, 'The Goddess of Sex will kill me! She'll destroy everything I have. Her voice is so loud in my ears! And it's too late—the damage is already done. Even Vaishali hates me now!'

In that instant, I realized something ghastly. The entire ordeal became clear before my eyes. I looked into his tear-soaked eyes and asked firmly, 'You tried it, didn't you? You tried to do... *vashikaran*.'

Manthan howled for several minutes like a helpless creature before finally composing himself. I wiped his tears as he whispered his story—a painful account of a young boy ensnared by the demons of blind faith.

An hour passed, then another. Finally, I rose after offering him a few words of comfort. He seemed lighter, calmer, and even managed a faint smile. I assured him, 'I will come back to you and end this vicious thing that has imprisoned you inside your own soul. I promise you.'

Before leaving, I told Mr Nagpal, 'Sir, I cannot tell you anything right now. But I will return and explain everything. I have only one request—Manthan feels better at the moment. Please don't ask him any more questions. Let him heal. I have a task to complete, and only then will his ordeal truly end.'

1 December 2018, Ujjain, Madhya Pradesh, 10.15 p.m.

Touched by the 'Goddess of Sex'

I sat on the bed in a hallucinatory state, while my senses wreaked havoc on my mind. I tried to get up, but couldn't. I slumped back onto the bed, struggling to focus my energies and regain consciousness.

As the dizziness slowly began to fade, I felt a strange euphoria rising within me—an unnatural force trying to ignite my sexual desire. My mortal frame made of flesh and blood, my own wretched body, fought a vicious battle against myself, *Jay Alani*—the man desperately leading a subconscious crusade against all that was foul. Finally, I understood that my inner will had managed to overpower the assault, but I was still perilously vulnerable.

And then, something else began to unfold before my eyes, threatening to defeat my fragile show of strength. It was *her*—Kamini, the 'Goddess of Sex'—with me inside that dingy, closed room. Strange neon lights flickered, while the cloying fragrance of attar, sprinkled over everything, choked the air.

She was in her late thirties, but her body had a voluptuous allure. The serpent tattoo on her shoulder lent her an even more brutal appearance. Her laughter was like the sting of some venomous creature from hell, a sound that pierced its prey with lust. Ooohhh…it was horrific!

Yet, above all else, it was the razor-sharp glint in her eyes—the unmistakable gaze of a succubus—what Indian mythology defines as a *yakshini*. She came closer, sat beside me, and kissed my arms and shoulder. Her touch was unbearable, and I shuddered in shock.

As her laughter echoed through the room, I demanded in a choked voice, 'What have you… I mean, what was mixed in the water I drank? Tell me!'

She rose in a flash, her body twisting into a provocative posture. With a poisonous whisper, she began to undress. Standing completely naked before me, she hissed, 'It is the potion from heaven!'

Then she stepped closer and declared, 'Sahib, inside this locked room, you must prove your manhood in bed with the Goddess of Sex! Yes—that's me, Kamini. This occult ritual is mandatory. And as you reach the peak of our union, you must see whether your seed can float on the water without sinking! Do you desire your lady-love with passion? Then to conquer her heart, you must imprison her desires and her secret erotic persona so that she remains your slave. Tonight, I shall be an impersonation of her, and this ritual will be your first step to claim her soul…'

It was a moment of sheer, paralytic fear and shame. I closed my eyes. Within my heart and subconscious, I saw three faces that gave me strength—the faces of Baba, Maa and Priyanka.

I knew that as the crusader against blind faith, I stood on the brink of an apocalyptic battle. But I was not ready to accept defeat.

Five Days Ago

A Bizarre 'Godman' and His Evil 'Goddess'

I had found my next mission—to chase the reality of vashikaran in India. My experience with Manthan had left me shaken, revealing how deeply these occult practices had permeated society with their poisonous ideas and false promises. Vashikaran, for me, was uncharted territory, and a dangerous one. The traps laid through this type of spell-casting have countless hidden risks. Yet, the ever-renewing permutations of human desire have made people—especially young people of this century—more and more vulnerable to such hateful practices.

But I knew I had to leap into that fire. From my conversations with Manthan, I managed to extract a few facts.

First, Manthan, a shy college student, had a crush on his neighbour Vaishali. Yet he had never mustered the courage to express his feelings.

Second, during a recent excursion to Ujjain in Madhya Pradesh, Manthan was trapped by a villainous gang of devotees who followed a tantric who claimed to be their supreme leader.

Third, in a secret occult ritual, Manthan had been forced to confront someone who posed as Kamini, the so-called Goddess of Sex.

Fourth, after returning to Delhi, Manthan followed the tantric's instructions. He carried out acts that strained his relationship with Vaishali even further. Worse, he was given something to consume by the tantric. Over time, this led to his strange fears and hallucinations.

Fifth, after a lot of hesitation and pleading, Manthan finally revealed the name of this so-called supreme leader: Baba Dayanand of Ujjain, the city of Mahakal.

Before proceeding further, I began my research and secured my contacts so the mission would have a higher chance of success. I reached out to Rohit—the one person I knew could help me. Rohit had been an admirer of my work—a loyal follower who had been in touch with me ever since he became a fan of my podcast. He was a resident of Ujjain, and worked as an agent for pilgrims. Every day, countless devotees throng the sacred Mahakal Temple, and they often rely on agents like him for accommodation, ritual arrangements and travel.

Rohit was an expert at his job. With years of experience, he had contacts everywhere in the city. I was certain he could connect me to my target and also provide crucial information. More importantly, his help would ensure a measure of safety for me.

When I called him, Rohit responded eagerly. As expected, he made every arrangement. In return for my appreciation, he said with excitement, 'Sir, the bonus for me is this golden opportunity to finally meet you!'

Armed with information about this hideous nexus, I prepared myself to confront the dangers of these repugnant practices. A few days later, I reached Ujjain. After checking into a hotel, I met Rohit. Though it was our first face-to-face meeting, he instantly felt like a worthy companion, guide and friend.

It was late evening, but I was determined to speak with the godman Baba Dayanand. As we sat down for dinner at a restaurant, Rohit handed me a phone number. I dialled it.

Baba Dayanand answered in a sombre voice.

'Baba,' I said smoothly, 'I am Mayank Kapoor from Delhi, here to seek your blessings. There is something troubling me—something that has caused me immense pain and heartache. Please help me.'

The voice responded, laced with a subtle, hypnotic villainy: 'Son, don't worry. I can understand—it's a case of love, isn't it? You want the companionship of the girl you desire. Right?'

His cunning tone was unmistakable. I played along, replying politely, 'Yes, Baba! You are great. You can read my heart and mind. Now, please help me.'

'Don't panic,' Baba Dayanand said. 'Come to my den tomorrow evening at 7.00. Remember, you must fast the entire day. Only fruits are allowed. You may drink water or milk, nothing else. Take a bath, wear fresh clothes, and then come to me. This ritual will cost ₹25,000—bring the cash with you up front. I trust that will be fine?'

I assented and disconnected the call.

Rohit and I finished a sumptuous dinner. Before parting ways, he leaned closer and whispered, 'Jay Sir, please be careful. These are dangerous men, with a network that has connections in powerful and influential circles. Baba Dayanand is not someone to be underestimated.'

1 December 2018, 9.30 p.m.

Meeting Baba Dayanand

At 6.30 that evening, I reached the outskirts of the city, near a semi-dense forest. Rohit dropped me at the highway and said he would pick me up from the same spot at dawn. I bid him goodbye and walked in the direction he had given me.

A five-minute walk brought me to the hideous tantric den. It was a shady cluster of huts, at the centre of which sat a man. One of his accomplices approached me, and I told him, 'My name is Mayank. I spoke with Baba last night through a local agent called Rohit.'

The man studied me carefully, then led me to their leader. Baba Dayanand was seated in front of a sacrificial fire, in the middle of a meditative ritual. I was asked to wash my hands and feet, then sit inside a large circle drawn on the ground. I followed the instructions and sat.

Baba Dayanand sat directly in front of me. Bare-bodied and wearing only a loincloth, he had a long grey beard and a massive plaited jata piled atop his head. He looked formidable. But it was his deep, red eyes—with their hypnotic glow—that radiated a magnetic charisma.

The illustrious, self-proclaimed godman listened to my plea once more and then said, 'The ancient method of vashikaran can turn one's target into a puppet. One becomes capable of making the person do anything through supernatural and paranormal means. It is a process of casting a powerful spell to subjugate your target to your will.'

I sat listening to his gibberish, pretending to be mesmerized. He continued:

'Mayank, remember—just as the way to a man's soul is

through his stomach, the way to a woman's soul is through her genitalia! Yes…it is true. Conquer that path, and the woman will be yours forever. She will never betray you. She will always belong to you. In this tantric ritual, you must attain supreme power to gain victory in that conquest.'

He paused, handed me a metal bowl and a glass of water, then said, 'Take this vial of holy oil. Go inside that room and rub it on your entire body. Yes—every part of your body. I trust that you understand? Then drink the holy water in this glass. After that, wait for the ritual to begin…'

He resumed chanting strange mantras, sprinkling flower petals and pinches of vibhuti over me. As I sat there witnessing this senseless charade, I was shocked. My heart screamed: '*This villain is telling me that a woman must be sexually abused and assaulted to win her love! This is atrocious and evil. Isn't there anything called love in this world? Is love only defined by physical desire? Is the bond between a man and woman governed only by their genitals? No! No! No, this can't be! This is nothing but an eyewash to spread blind faith, and fool innocent people. If life has meaning, if there is any truth in this universe, if the paranormal has a purpose—then this is a lie. This is a desecration of womanhood. A dishonour to every mother. I will not tolerate this.*'

Determined, I rose to my feet. One of the accomplices showed me the way, and I entered the room. He closed the door from the outside.

The atmosphere inside was dingy, illuminated by harsh green neon lights and heavy with the overpowering fragrance of attar. The room reeked of artificiality. Other than a bed and a small table with a bowl of water, it was bare.

To feign compliance, I rubbed some of the oil on

my hands, neck and feet, and then set the vial aside. Its strong menthol-like stench was nauseating. To suppress my queasiness, I drank the water Baba Dayanand had offered me.

That was a grave mistake. Within minutes, a strange sensation gripped my body. I felt intoxicated. Obsessed with uncovering the truth, I had unwittingly consumed water laced with some drug. I felt weak, sweat trickled down my face, and the hallucinations took over.

Oh no! This is bad…very bad. What will happen now? Fear clawed at me. For the first time during this investigation, I was truly afraid. But the worst was yet to come.

Moments later, the door opened. A woman stepped inside. She smiled, locked the door from within, and turned towards me.

'Let us begin and finish the ritual,' she said.

I looked at her—and realized that my deepest fear was about to come alive.

1 December 2018, 11.25 p.m.

An Apocalyptic Battle of 'Faith' and a 'Curse'

Kamini extended her delicate hands and touched my face. I recoiled, shrugging them off in deep abhorrence. Then I rose. Yes, I had found the inner strength within me, drawn from the vision of my loved ones. I stood and looked into her eyes.

Kamini smirked and said, 'So, are you ready? Come, embrace me, and prove your—'

'Stop!' I protested, my voice firm and unshaken. 'I cannot do this. This is not what I believe in. This is not my "faith", it is a "curse", and I refuse to accept it.'

Kamini shamelessly tried to press her body against mine and retorted, 'You dare deny the goddess who resides within me?' she shrieked. 'I am the Goddess of sex incarnate. How else will your desires be fulfilled?'

'Dear lady,' I said, staggering slightly as I walked towards the door. 'I don't need to worship you. And you are no goddess.'

For a fleeting moment, a shadow of remorse flickered in her eyes, but she quickly concealed it. She picked up her clothes while said in a strong and steady voice: 'It is humans who commit misdeeds, and yet the blame is thrust upon God. Remember this—no goddess needs to mate with a mortal to bestow blessings. Such acts can only be done by…'

I stopped myself from uttering an abuse. I controlled my temper and said, 'The so-called potion from heaven has lost its effect. It cannot force me to stoop to something I don't believe in. Leave me alone.'

With that, I opened the door and walked out. That night, I longed to confront Baba Dayanand and expose his villainy, but Rohit's words of caution echoed in my mind. Moreover, I still needed to uncover what exactly was done to Manthan. Deep inside, I strongly believed that Manthan had not succumbed to that woman's filthy proposal either.

And so I waited patiently.

1 December 2018, 12.30 a.m.

The 'Baba' and his 'Vashikaran'

'Baba,' I exhaled, like a man gasping for breath, 'I cannot do this ritual. Please tell me if you know another method to fulfil my desire.'

Baba Dayanand looked at me and said, 'Give the ₹25,000 to him.'

He pointed towards one of his accomplices, and I did so obediently. I didn't want to enrage him. As the man counted the money, nodded, and went away, Baba Dayanand said, 'There is one last path to do this, but you must follow exactly what I say. Can you?'

I gave my consent, and he continued, 'Take this bottle. It contains a sacred potion. Go back home and divide it into two equal portions. Drink one teaspoon of it every night before going to sleep for 10 days. It will invigorate you and give you power. Then, on the thirteenth day, take your girl to a secluded place and make her drink the other half. If she doesn't consent, mix it with something and give it to her. The power of the sacred potion will make her yours! She will submit herself to you, and you must seek the path to her soul, just as I told you earlier. Ahhhh…then the job will be done!'

I obediently accepted the bottle. This was what I had been waiting for—my weapon to expose these goons and prove that, in the name of God, they were nothing more than filthy drug-peddlers. He sprinkled some water on me, laughed like a Devil, and said, 'God bless you! Now, go and rest for a while. At dawn, you must leave.'

The rest of the night passed quickly as I sat in a corner, watching their bizarre rituals, while those villainous men indulged in drunken revelry. At one point, I turned my eyes towards the huts and saw that evil woman lurking in a corner, devouring food and collecting money from one of the men.

I sighed to myself, *'So this is the world of gods and goddesses that contaminates our society. A world that we humans have created.'*

Amidst all of this—despite being drugged and abused—I had accomplished a secret task. The tiny hidden sound recorder in my pocket had remained safe, capturing every single conversation I had with them that night.

4 December 2018, 10.35 a.m.

One Last Visit to the 'Goddess of Sex'

The next morning, I went back to the hotel. Rohit picked me up from the exact spot where he had dropped me. That morning, I didn't utter a single word. Before going into the hotel, I asked Rohit to meet me three hours later.

When Rohit returned, I said, 'I just need one last favour. Will you do it for the sake of humanity?'

He nodded in agreement, carefully listened to my audacious request, and left.

Two days later, I found myself in the slums on the outskirts of Ujjain. Rohit and I walked through the twisting lanes crowded with innumerable shacks until we arrived at the one we were looking for. A little ten-year-old girl was playing outside.

I smiled at her and asked, 'What is your name?'

'Phulwari,' she replied softly.

I pulled out a piece of chocolate and gave it to her with my love and blessings. The innocence in her eyes stirred something within me. We began chatting with our little friend. As our voices reached inside, a woman emerged from the shack. Her voice called out, 'Who are you talking to?'

'She is talking to me… Kamini,' I replied firmly, meeting her eyes and silencing her. Then I added, 'Is that your real name? So is this your truth? Is this the truth of the goddess? Should I tell your child—and everyone else in this neighbourhood—the truth?'

The woman's eyes welled with tears. The look on her face changed from horror to pain, and then to repentance. Folding her hands in supplication, she begged silently. I nodded, and she took Rohit and me to an empty park beside the slums. There, she confessed:

'Sahib, forgive me. Please don't say anything to anybody here. And please spare my little daughter! I beg you… Baba Dayanand is a villain! He is an imposter who fools innocent victims. After my husband died, I became a helpless widow with no income. So I chose to become one of his accomplices. My role is to lure people who surrender to their desires and to engage in shameful acts with them that are part of the so-called occult rituals Baba Dayanand conducts. Some men become so obsessed that they keep returning for a night with the "Goddess of Sex". Then we begin to blackmail them or extort money through other means. Sahib, it is unfortunate but true. I am no goddess. I am just a poor woman! And whenever that evil Baba Dayanand wishes to fulfil his own sexual desires, I must be his muse. Please forgive me…'

'You have no excuse for engaging in such acts of wickedness,' I replied sternly. 'It is a crime, and you are a criminal. You could have chosen a life that was tougher but far more respectful. I hope you will do so in the future.'

She sobbed and nodded. I felt pity, but pressed on, 'Now tell me something. Did a young boy from Delhi, named Manthan, visit Baba Dayanand's den a few weeks ago? Did you make him indulge in the evil act?'

'Yes,' she admitted quietly. 'He came. But he was too afraid to do anything. He was inside the room with me, and as I approached him, he began to cry. So I asked him to leave. Baba Dayanand gave him a bottle of the sacred potion and he went away.'

I had no more questions. Before turning to leave, I pulled out some money, handed it to her, and said, 'I don't know your real name—and I don't want to. Take this money and try to build a decent life for yourself. Phulwari is a beautiful child. Give her a good life, and protect her from the shadows of this evil.'

As we left the slums, I felt a quiet satisfaction. Not only had I uncovered the truth, but my little hidden sound recorder had once again done a good job.

8 December 2018, Pitampura, New Delhi

The Showdown

Sitting inside Manthan's room, I played the audio files on my computer. Manthan listened to everything in silence, utterly speechless. Then I took out a piece of paper and handed it to him. It was the chemical analysis report of the liquid that Baba Dayanand had given me.

I said, 'The liquid that Baba Dayanand gave you—and me—contains a drug called gamma-hydroxybutyric acid. It is a naturally occurring neurotransmitter as well as a psychoactive drug. It's a depressant that affects the central nervous system. It is commonly known as a club drug or a date-rape drug. It causes hallucinations, making your brain bring your worst fears to life. It usually comes as a liquid or a white powder that can be dissolved in water, juice or alcohol.'

As tears rolled down his cheeks, I continued, 'Manthan, you are a good human being. I know everything now, and you must also know that you were duped by a fake baba and drugged without your knowledge. The Goddess of Sex is nothing but a cunning trap to ensnare victims. Thankfully, you were spared from the full ordeal. Unfortunately, the drug wreaked havoc on your consciousness and made you hallucinate that evil woman with the serpent tattoo.'

Manthan looked ashamed and kept silent. I sat beside him and said gently, 'I also spoke with Vaishali. She told me everything. And after learning how you became a victim of those villains, she has chosen to forgive you. She doesn't hate you anymore for trying to spike her soft drink with that liquid on your first date. She understands how much you love her, and how much an innocent man like you needs the support and love of a mature girl like her.'

For the first time, Manthan lifted his head and smiled. Then he said, 'Really? Is that true, Jay Sir? Thank you so much. I am so ashamed of my deeds. But I promise I shall never do anything foolish again. Did… Vaishali really forgive me?'

'Yes,' I smiled back. 'Now cheer up and get ready. She will be waiting for you for your second date. This time, my brother, make it special—with love that is true.'

I opened the door and asked Mr Nagpal to come inside. As he hugged his grandchild, I said, 'Love is a complex emotion that resides within the heart. It is divine and cannot be explained with logic. Love makes this world beautiful. That is why the world of literature is filled with timeless stories of romance. And those are not just tales of love between a man and a woman, but also tales of love among families, friends and human souls.'

Mr Arvind Nagpal thanked me with the innocence of a child, but I said, 'Sir, it was my duty, and I am glad I could do it well. Manthan had been a victim of a vicious gang of lunatics who practise villainy in the name of vashikaran. I am happy he has overcome it now.'

My work, my mission, my crusade—to eliminate blind faith and establish paranormal reality—shall continue to drive me to do the unthinkable. That is my destiny.

That day, after walking out of Mr Nagpal's house, I came home and deleted the audio files.

Rohit's earnest request echoed in my ears, and I destroyed all evidence of the case. Yes, I had saved one life—Manthan's, but I didn't proceed to hunt down Baba Dayanand. Why? The reason wasn't simple.

I honoured Rohit's request because I was worried about his safety. He had said, 'Jay Sir, I am taking you to this woman's shack so that you can uncover their crimes. But Sir, if you reveal their identity to the world, the treacherous gang will surely know that I was the whistle-blower. Baba Dayanand has deep pockets and roots buried deep inside the world of crime. They will kill me!'

'Don't worry, Rohit,' I replied. 'I shall not let any harm come to you.'

Even though I destroyed the proof, I vowed to myself that I would speak about the evil nexus on my podcast so that more people could learn the truth. It is unfortunate that today the internet, social media, newspapers and magazines are inundated with advertisements from such fake wizards and godmen who claim to possess the power of casting spells.

It is shameful that in our modern society such evil people exist only because of our own avaricious nature.

Vashikaran is not a way to attain love or win someone's faith. These evil practices are designed to hurl innocent humans into the tunnel of hell.

7

My Evil Sister

'You're not my "best friend", you're my "sister" from the "abyss".'

Mid-January 2019, New Delhi, 9.23 p.m.

The Summons of an 'Evil Sister'

As I sat on the chair beside my bed, my mind went over the rollercoaster ride that was my life for the past few years. My journey from Patna to Mumbai as a vagabond, the relentless struggle that left me in a state of utter despondency, the emotional turmoil of my relationships, my desperate attempts to quit, and my final fight for survival in Delhi—all of it left a lasting mark on my being.

Yet that night, I could finally tell myself: *'The seeds of your efforts and struggles have begun to sprout!'*

My podcast—my first foray into the creative industry—was finally getting the recognition I had craved. *Paranormal Reality*, my unscripted podcast, had become a success. The OTT platform promoters agreed to give me a much-coveted opportunity, and I gave it everything I had. It had always been my principle to expose the truth behind paranormal events but never to charge money for any of my investigations. The stories themselves were a goldmine that I intended to explore creatively for a wider audience. The podcast gave me that chance.

Despite lacking hi-tech editing or elaborate background scores, the podcast was a phenomenal success. Its uniqueness lay in its raw, unscripted nature. The spontaneous narrative of unvarnished truth lent it credibility. Within a short time, it garnered millions of views! My name gained some recognition too. The once-anonymous Jay Alani was now being noticed by the media. Newspaper features and talk-show invitations started coming in.

My heart was content as I prepared for Season 2, following the acclaim of Season 1. My dream was slowly becoming a reality. Yet, despite its popularity, the podcast didn't bring significant financial gains. My regular job supplemented my income, allowing me a modest but decent lifestyle.

Still, that night, a strange uneasiness lingered in my heart. It had gripped me ever since SHE left that afternoon. Yes—*she*. My cousin Isha…or should I say, *my evil sister*!

Before I could dwell on it, my phone buzzed. It was an Instagram notification. That wasn't unusual—every day I received messages from people seeking my help to deal with their paranormal experiences.

This one read:

'Dear Mr Jay, my name is Manu. I am from Guwahati. I know of your work as a paranormal investigator, so I am reaching out to you…'

Then came another message:

'Sir, I desperately need your help! I'm certain the soul of my deceased sister has returned from Hell to haunt us! She's here—

she's everywhere. If nothing is done soon...she will kill us all.'

The words sent a chill down my spine. The mention of 'sister' only heightened the uneasiness that was already gnawing at me. My instincts pushed me to respond.

I typed out my phone number and replied, *'Manu, here is my contact. Call me immediately.'*

The message was delivered but went unread. I waited for his call with a pounding heart.

Flashback: The Morning of the Same Day

Isha, my cousin, had always been much more than a sister. Through the different phases of my life, she appeared in many forms—sometimes a sister, sometimes a confidante, and in my most turbulent times, she showered me with the motherly love my heart longed for. She was an emotional constant in my ever-changing life—a pillar of support who stayed with me through thick and thin.

A week earlier, she had arrived in Delhi to attend a friend's wedding. During her week-long stay at my apartment, our conversations often drifted towards the burning issues in my life.

'Jay, how is the podcast going?' she asked on the second evening after her arrival, as we sipped coffee, enjoying the chilly winter winds.

'It's gaining tremendous success,' I replied, a smile spreading across my face. 'I'm finally happy that my work is getting the recognition it deserves.'

'Are you making enough money?' Isha pressed.

The question was uncomfortable but inevitable. I smiled wryly. 'Well, to be honest, no. The podcast has a huge viewership, but my earnings are meagre. Thankfully, my regular job covers the gap.'

'That's not enough for you to survive in the long run, Jay,' she said, irritation creeping into her voice.

'Isha, my dreams have never been too lofty,' I explained. 'Yes, I'd like a car—even a small one. A house—even if it's in the suburbs. But above all, my mission matters more. That comes first.'

Isha thought for a moment before suggesting, 'Why don't you start something of your own? Your own podcast channel, maybe even an OTT app for your paranormal investigations? It could boost your earnings. And Jay, you need to start using advanced gadgets too. Paranormal investigators across the globe use them to build their credibility. You need to modernize your approach.'

I already knew my answer. 'Isha, gadgets can never replace human instincts. I firmly believe that the human quotient is far more important than any device. Technology can assist you, but it can't replace the human mind. Many so-called paranormal cases turn out to be instances of blind faith or psychological disorders. My aim is to help people, not sensationalize their suffering as ghost stories.'

Deep down, I knew Isha's idea of starting my own OTT platform was ambitious, maybe too ambitious. It would require significant funding, infrastructure and time. And if I turned my mission into a full-fledged business, I feared that commercial demands would crush the very purpose behind it.

Perhaps Isha sensed my hesitation. 'We could try approaching a few investors,' she offered. 'Maybe it will work, maybe it won't. But there's no harm in trying.'

For the next six days, our conversations kept circling around similar themes. Isha had always been protective of me, sometimes to the point of possessiveness.

Finally, the day came when she had to leave. As we sat waiting for her cab that afternoon, she turned to me and said, 'Jay, I don't think Priyanka is the right person for you. She doesn't deserve you.'

She was visibly upset about my relationship with Priyanka—especially about how uncertain everything seemed despite the years we had been together.

'Why is there no concrete plan?' she demanded. 'If Priyanka truly loves you, why is she so hesitant? Your financial position shouldn't be stopping her. She should convince her parents, she should stand up for you. Why is she so unsure?'

I had no answers. Yes, Priyanka loved me, and I loved her deeply. But I couldn't explain to Isha why things weren't moving faster. A part of me worried she might speak to my parents and complicate things further. Isha's concerns were valid, but her perception felt wrong.

Then she said the words that shattered me: 'Jay, you should end this relationship. It has no future. Be practical. This is the right time to say goodbye to her.'

That was it. I ran out of patience. I yelled at her, venting all the frustration I had kept bottled inside. Isha sat frozen as I lashed out. She hadn't expected this storm. Then silently, with tears in her eyes, she rose, grabbed her luggage, and walked out. The cab had arrived. She got in without another word. Our eyes didn't meet. I kept sitting in silence as she shut the car door.

But as the cab began to move, something inside me

cracked. I rushed out and shouted, 'Isha, it's time for us to say goodbye to each other!'

And in that instant, in the heat of the moment and in anger and heartbreak, she transformed into…*my evil sister.*

New Delhi, 10.38 p.m., That Same Night

A 'Lethal Riddle' Continues

I had been waiting for two long hours. Manu didn't call. My restless mind kept playing games with my subconscious—a concoction of grief, rage, fear and anxiety. The shocking argument with Isha was still fresh in my mind, and my apprehensions about nightmares gnawed at me from within. I looked at my watch. It was 10.38 p.m. Closing my eyes, I wished for Manu to call me.

Then, at that precise moment, the cell-phone rang. As I answered, a male voice spoke. 'Hi Jay, this is Manu from Guwahati.'

'Hi Manu,' I said. 'I saw your message, and an uncanny impulse is compelling me to know more. Please tell me everything. I need every intricate detail to be in a position to help you.'

Manu replied, 'Yes, Jay. I will do that. This is about my sister Ashi. She is no more. She's dead.'

A chill ran down my spine as he uttered those words. Isha's face flashed through my mind, and I tried to brush off all my negative thoughts. Deep within the recesses of my subconscious, I even felt an urge to call her to make sure she had reached home safely.

Manu continued his tale.

Ashi was two years younger than me. She was my beloved little angel. We were a family of four—Baba, Maa, Ashi and me. We lived on the outskirts of Guwahati, about 70 km from the city, in a nondescript village called Rongmaja. Jay, we were a happy family, very happy!

We belonged to an affluent stratum of society. We had a big house, stretches of cropland, and a solid financial status thanks to our foundation in agriculture. Local villagers called our house the 'haveli'. The four of us lived happily, and Ashi and I grew up in a beautiful and loving home. Yes, we were rich by rural standards, but we were also content and well respected. There were no negatives in our lives—until the curse struck.

The fateful day when the heinous curse struck our family is still etched in my memory. It happened about eight years ago. Ashi was 17 and I was 19. Why it happened—why we were chosen by God or the devil for such devastation—I still don't know.

Our cropland was a few kilometres from our house, stretching across open fields. After sunset, it became very dark in those secluded areas. However, our village was peaceful, and it was generally safe to go out even in that darkness.

That day, Baba was in Guwahati for urgent work. So Maa, Ashi and I were on our own. As darkness fell, I sat and waited for them to come home. To be precise, I was in the Haveli while Ashi and Maa were in the fields. The night was moonless. The stars twinkled in the sky, and no one else was in sight.

Maa was hurriedly walking a few paces ahead of Ashi when she suddenly heard a thud. In that vast emptiness, the sound amplified manifold. She stopped and turned around quickly, only to be shocked. Ashi was lying unconscious on the ground—she had fainted all of a sudden!

Maa could not find any reason behind it. She ran to her and tried to wake her up. Her howls went unheard as she struggled to bring Ashi back to consciousness. When her efforts failed, Maa used all her strength, picked Ashi up, and dragged her home.

As they arrived, I ran to help them. I was too shocked at the unthinkable sight. Maa and I brought her inside and took her to her bedroom. She came to after we splashed plenty of water on her face, but it was only momentary. Soon, she fell asleep again.

The next morning, Baba returned. Ashi remained in a trance. She had a fever and slept for hours. The usually chirpy and mischievous girl had suddenly turned to stone. Baba and Maa were worried. I went out to seek help from the local doctor. He arrived, saw Ashi, and prescribed some medicines. Maa administered them diligently, but Ashi's continued to sleep for long stretches of time for the next three or four days. She remained in a state of slumber, and her fever stayed high.

After five days of treatment, Ashi improved. However, something had changed deep within her. I could feel it in my heart. My little sister was no longer the same person I had known since birth. As siblings, we were very close, as were our parents, yet this drastic metamorphosis was unnerving.

The strangest episodes began a few days later. Ashi's behaviour became alien. I never spoke about it, but I could sense a bad omen. I was terrified.

At night, Ashi would wake up and silently sneak to the roof, alone, for hours. At first, nobody noticed. But a few days later, I saw her walking up the stairs in the darkness. There was something eerie in her gait—it was as if she were floating.

I followed her silently. In that dark night, shrouded in obscurity, I saw her standing near the parapet for almost two hours. She had a blank stare in her eyes. I was shocked and ran back to my room.

The following nights, the same episode repeated. Petrified, I informed Maa. One night, both Maa and I hid in a corner while Ashi came onto the roof. It was 2.00 a.m. She stood near the parapet, gazing at something far away in the fields. Our eyes couldn't penetrate the darkness to figure out what she was looking at. Then suddenly, Ashi began banging her head against the wall. Maa was terrified and wept. Ashi was unaware of our presence, as if she were hallucinating. She banged her hands and head on the wall until blood oozed out. Then she fainted.

Maa and I ran across the roof, picked her up, and brought her to her room. Maa administered first aid and treated her wounds. We were extremely worried. We sealed the door to the roof, but to our shock, in the next two nights, Ashi unlocked the front door and wandered into the fields. I followed her on the second night and found her standing at a corner of the cropland, motionless, her eyes fixed on something invisible.

The next night, Baba instructed the servants to chain the front door shut. He was due to travel to Guwahati for two days. That night, nothing happened. Ashi stayed in her room. Maa and I felt relieved.

Around noon the following day, I was sitting in the courtyard, and Maa was in the kitchen, when the fateful incident occurred. 'Eeeee!' Ashi's scream exploded through the house. Maa and I ran to her room and froze. The sight was ghastly. Maa screamed and clutched me tightly.

Manu paused. I could feel the apprehension building. Then he continued:

Ashi's entire body was floating horizontally in the air, almost a foot above the bed. It was as if the devil held her in his arms. Jay, I had never seen such horror. My hands and feet trembled with fear. Ashi's eyes rolled back, and she moaned in an unearthly fashioned that chilled our blood. Yet Maa and I gathered the courage, jumped on the bed, and held her tightly. Her body descended smoothly, but a gust of wind and a foul stench rushed from the room.

Ashi's state was pitiable. Her tongue was bleeding, and she was virtually trying to chew it off. It was a tormenting scene. We gave her sleeping pills and, after a great struggle, she finally fell asleep. After Baba returned, the doctor treated Ashi's tongue and gave her medicines. By then, it was clear to the three of us that Ashi was being haunted by a powerful paranormal entity.

With the help of a distant relative, we consulted a tantric. He observed Ashi and proclaimed that she was possessed by three evil spirits. The entities controlled her mind, body and soul. He admitted that their powers were far greater than his own. He performed some provisional rituals and left, cautioning us heavily.

None of us knew what awaited. That night was cursed. The morning revealed Ashi to have died in her sleep. Maa discovered her lifeless body. Baba and I rushed in. Jay, it was gruesome. Ashi's body had turned blue, as if poisoned. Maa collapsed; Baba sank into a deep depression. The police arrived, but the autopsy found nothing. Her death was marked as natural.

Jay, my little sister, my beloved angel, died a heinous death. Within a month, our happy world had turned into hell. We were shattered. Yet we didn't know it was just the beginning. Years later, life began to become normal again. Baba, Maa and I accepted the tragedy. But three years later, on a winter morning, Maa and I found Baba's lifeless body hanging from the ceiling. Our universe collapsed. Why? The question had no answer. I knew it—paranormal forces were behind it...

I interrupted Manu: 'Why do you think so? Were there reasons for your belief?'

Manu replied, 'Baba never had bouts of depression. He was always strong—the one who helped Maa recover. If he had intended to commit suicide, he would have done it soon after Ashi's death. Why wait three years? It made no sense.

'And there is something I never told anyone. After Ashi's demise, I felt an uncanny presence in the Haveli. I never saw it, but my senses guided me. Smell, touch, hearing and a sixth sense convinced me that Ashi never left the Haveli. She is omnipresent and roaming unnoticed, watching us. Her soul remained tethered to the Haveli, and she seeks something horrific.

'I know for certain—Ashi took Baba away. She caused his death. And she won't stop. She is here, even now, and one by one, she will kill everyone. Maa and I are next...'

As Manu finished recounting his ordeal, a heavy silence hung between us. In those moments, I turned inwards, reflecting on the enormity of the case. Seldom in the life of a paranormal investigator does such a case present itself. I was shaken by its intensity—shocking yet undeniably fascinating. My resolve intensified. I knew I had to get to the root of this critical situation.

It was a golden opportunity, and as a paranormal investigator, I couldn't let it slip away. I made my decision. I knew what my modus operandi would be. Though drained from hearing about the ordeal, I felt that it was my duty to act. I could not allow two more innocent lives to be claimed by whatever evil lurked in the Haveli.

Manu broke the silence with heartfelt sobs. 'Please, Jay. Please do something. I think Maa is the next victim! I cannot afford to lose her!'

I steadied him by putting my arms around him. 'Manu, I am coming immediately,' I said resolutely. 'Have faith in me. I will not let any more misfortune touch you. Please send me your address.'

Isha's face flashed before my eyes. A wave of melancholy overwhelmed me. Perhaps from her perspective, she was right. The hatred that had clouded my judgement slowly evaporated. I felt a sudden urge to speak with her. Then, in an uncanny coincidence, my cell-phone rang. It was Isha. Her familiar husky voice was nectar to my ears. 'I have reached home…'

I smiled, let out a soft sigh. 'Okay. Good night.'

3 Days Later, Guwahati, 10.15 p.m.

At the Haveli, 70 Kilometres Away

Over the past three days, I had dedicated all my energy to devising a concrete plan for how I would approach the case. I kept my mind open and resolved to treat Manu's account as the truth—at least until proved otherwise. I booked my tickets, packed my bags, and made preparations.

To uncover the reality behind the paranormal activity, I needed evidence. So I gathered all the necessary equipment, even though I knew that above all I would need to summon my inner strength to confront whatever haunted the place.

My flight reached Guwahati in the morning. From the airport, I hired a cab and headed straight to the Haveli.

The first glimpse of the mansion left me awestruck. It was an enormous structure, easily big enough to house 50 people. The central verandah was surrounded by rooms on all sides, spread across two storeys. A sprawling hallway connected nearly every room. Manu told me the house was almost 75 years old, yet it was remarkably well maintained.

Outside, I noticed two motorbikes and three cars—all belonging to the family. Clearly, their financial standing remained strong. Manu, his mother, and a trusted servant named Bholu lived in this sprawling ancestral home.

Manu and his mother welcomed me warmly.

'Jay,' Manu asked hesitantly, 'could you please tell me about your charges?'

I smiled. 'Manu, I don't charge my clients for these investigations. If I can help you, that will be my reward. My mission is to eradicate blind faith and uncover paranormal reality. I firmly believe the world of spirits is far more complex than what people usually imagine. That's the message I want to spread. Now, let's focus on the problem at hand.'

After some tea and conversation, I requested their permission to inspect every inch of the Haveli. Manu readily agreed, and for nearly two hours, he guided me through every corner of the old mansion. I carefully scrutinized each room, paying special attention to the bedrooms that once belonged to Ashi and her father.

Later, over dinner, I spoke to Manu. 'I've chalked out a plan,' I said. 'But I'll need your permission to execute it.'

Manu nodded for me to continue.

'For the next three days,' I explained, 'I need to conduct a thorough investigation inside the Haveli. For this, I'll require privacy. Please send your mother to stay elsewhere during this period. Only you, Bholu, and I should remain here. And I'll need complete freedom to move about the house at any hour. This is essential for the investigation to succeed.'

Manu agreed without any hesitation. 'Tomorrow morning, I'll take Maa to my aunt's house in Guwahati. I'll return to join you by afternoon. In the meantime, Bholu will assist you.'

The first night passed quietly. I spent my time drafting a detailed blueprint of the Haveli and noting down everything I had learnt from Manu, his mother and Bholu. I filled my notebook, trying to identify patterns in the strange events that had taken place. Outside, the night was dark and cold. The chilly wind whistled like a restless spirit.

Around midnight, I slipped out of my room and climbed to the roof. Everyone else was asleep. Even in the open air, I felt a strange dampness—as though I had entered a closed, forgotten room after many years. A few minutes later, an unshakeable feeling crept over me. My spine tingled.

Someone—or something—was watching me.

I stood there, wrapped in darkness, and spoke softly into the night. 'Whoever is here, I have come to seek the truth.'

I closed my eyes and exhaled deeply, letting the fear leave with my breath.

For 15 long minutes, I waited. Nothing happened. Finally, I descended the stairs, returned to my room, and drifted into sleep.

Investigation (Day–1)

'Hide & Seek'

The next morning, Manu left with his Maa, while Bholu remained with me. Throughout the day, I tested different spots, searching for the best places to set up the night-vision cameras. These sophisticated devices were equipped with motion sensors capable of detecting even the slightest movements—things invisible to the human eye.

By late afternoon, I was satisfied with the spots I had chosen. I placed the cameras in five key locations: the first in Ashi's room, the second in her Baba's room where he had taken his life, the third in the verandah, the fourth in the hallway that led to the staircase to the roof, and the fifth at the main entrance.

With this setup, I had eyes on almost every corner of the Haveli. I also placed thermal sensors and high-sensitivity sound amplifiers in each of these locations to capture fluctuations in temperature and sound. The EMF meter remained with me at all times. In my room, my computer was ready to record every reading. Yet deep inside, I knew that no gadget would reveal the truth on its own—something more human was required to reach a conclusion.

By evening, Manu returned. We discussed my plan over dinner, and as night fell, I gave clear instructions:

'Let's all stay in our respective rooms and behave as if it's a normal night. I'll keep watch, and so must the two of you. Whatever happens, do not fall asleep. We can't afford to miss even the slightest sign.'

After a final conversation, we retired to our rooms. I sat glued to the computer screen. For two hours, nothing happened.

Then I glanced at my watch—it was 1.12 a.m. The EMF meter in my hand flickered. The electromagnetic readings were higher than usual. I felt a faint throbbing in my chest.

I stepped out to check the thermal readings. Three devices registered a temperature drop, but I reminded myself that such changes were normal during a winter night, especially in a sprawling Haveli in the middle of a village.

Ten minutes later, I returned to my room. The long wait was unbearable. Still, that uneasy feeling of being watched grew more intense with each passing minute. Sweat gathered on my forehead, though I forced myself to remain calm.

Another hour passed. I decided to check on Manu and Bholu.

In the small room near the kitchen, I found Bholu reading a local magazine, struggling to keep his eyes open. I tapped his shoulder, signalling him to stay alert, and moved on.

Manu's room was eerily silent. Something about it unsettled me. In the dim light, I saw a shadow—a human silhouette. Like lightning, I rushed inside. Manu stood frozen, his eyes wide open. The shadow was his own, yet his body trembled uncontrollably.

I grabbed his shoulders and shook him. Slowly, he returned to his senses and whispered in a petrified voice, 'Jay… I just… I just heard her cry out.'

'What kind of cry?' I asked quickly.

'The same cry Ashi let out on that fateful day. I heard it clearly. Please help me, Jay. I don't want to die. I don't want Maa to die. Ashi's demonic spirit has returned to kill us.'

I calmed him and led him to my room, asking Bholu to stay with him. Then I rushed to check the sound amplifier recordings.

But nothing unusual had been captured.

It was 4 a.m. when I returned to Manu. Sitting beside him, I held his trembling hands. The warmth comforted him, and he wept like a child. We stayed awake until the first rays of dawn crept into the Haveli. Exhausted, the three of us ate a light breakfast before collapsing into sleep.

I knew one thing: though the first night had not given me any hard evidence, it had not been in vain. Something was close—very close.

The game of hide and seek had just begun.

Investigation (Day 2)

The Hunter and the Bait

Throughout the second day, I kept deliberating on what I could do differently in this mission. I wanted to apply what I had learnt from the first night. Only two days remained, and I needed to complete my task within that time.

A persistent thought echoed through my mind and soul: *'If this haunting is real, there is more than one presence in this Haveli. The spirits of Ashi and her Baba are not the only lingering energies here. Perhaps something far more demonic rules over this mansion—something that remains invisible.'*

After much thought, I concluded: *'If there is truly a paranormal entity here, it is revealing itself only to Manu. If he speaks the truth, then I must use that as my chance.'*

I made my decision: *'Tonight, Manu will be my bait. A hunter must use the best bait to capture his prey. I cannot tell him this, or he will be paralysed with fear. He must unknowingly become a volunteer in this dangerous game. To confront the entity that destroyed Ashi and her Baba, I must put Manu in its path.'*

Our routine began soon after dinner. By 11.00 p.m., we were inside my room. I connected the sound boosters to my earphones so that no noise could escape me. I handed a few gadgets to Manu and asked him to walk slowly around the veranda, the hallway, and near his own room. Then I waited—locked in nail-biting suspense.

Hours passed. Nothing.

By 5.15 a.m., we gave up our vigil. I was baffled. I had been so sure that something would happen, yet the night ended in silence. I had no explanation. Inside my head, a mocking voice whispered: '*You fool. This is no ordinary enemy. It knows you are here to confront it. Demonic energies cannot be defeated so easily.*'

Only one night remained. I said nothing to Manu, though I could see his disappointment. The final night would be critical. I gathered every ounce of strength to face what was to come.

Investigation (Day-3)

The Armageddon

The third night was meant for drastic action. I told Manu, 'Tonight, take your devices and reach the farthest corners of the house. If there is any place you suspect, go there without any fear. I'll observe everything and cover you if anything happens. I'll keep my eyes on you every moment.'

It was about 11.55 p.m. when Manu, carrying his gadgets, disappeared into the house. I sat in my room, intently focused on the readings. With all my senses sharpened to the highest level, I felt a strange current of energy running through me.

Then…it happened.

Without any warning, the lights went out. The power was gone. And then, from the darkness, a deep weeping sound crashed into my ears. The unearthly moan of a woman was so unnerving that every hair on my body stood on end. The cry—raw and hellish—pierced my heart for a few agonizing seconds before it stopped abruptly. With trembling hands, I replayed the recordings from the sound amplifiers. Yes…it was there. Without a shred of doubt, the cry was real.

Like a madman, I skimmed through the computer, desperate to trace the source. To my utter horror, I discovered that it was coming from a point very close to Manu. Goosebumps rippled across my skin, and I froze. My greatest fear had come true. I bolted from the room.

I dashed across the hallway and verandah. Both Manu and I had head-lamps strapped on, their beams cutting through the darkness. In that faint light, I found him. He looked at me, startled.

'What happened, Jay? Is everything alright?' he asked.

Panting heavily, I forced myself to calm my voice. 'Yes, Manu. Everything's fine. I think you should return to my room and take over the vigil. Meanwhile, I want to spend some time in Ashi's room.'

The request was born out of desperation. Manu led me there and then left. The torchlight still glowed—the electricity had not returned. I looked around. This was the room where Ashi was consumed by the haunting.

I sat down on the bed and lit a cigarette. It was the very bed where the demonic force had taken her life. The air was thick, damp and heavy—the same oppressive atmosphere as before. Once again, I sensed the gaze of unseen eyes upon me, burning into my back.

It was 3.11 a.m. A strange thought crept into my mind: *as if I had always known this Haveli…as if I belonged here.* The place seemed hauntingly familiar. Perhaps I was being possessed. I didn't understand—but I felt it.

A wave of exhaustion swept over me. My body weakened. Reclining on the bed, my eyes closed against my will, and I slipped into sleep. I was unprepared for what followed.

In that untimely slumber, the nightmare engulfed me. A dense mist rose and filled the room. A strange glow illuminated the darkness. Then, from within the mist, a girl floated into view. Her skin was pale, her eyes hollow, her face a mask of deathly blankness. She drifted soundlessly across the room—and then lunged.

I awoke with a start, drenched in terror. My heart hammered. I understood—it was a sign. The spirits were making their presence known. And in that moment, realization struck me: Manu was never the bait for the demonic spirit. I was.

No gadget could capture what my soul had just witnessed. Horror and ecstasy collided within me. I stumbled out of the room and into mine where Manu sat, his face pale and lifeless. I looked into his eyes and asked softly, 'Manu…is she here with us? Is Ashi here?'

He nodded once—and collapsed.

I shouted for help. Bholu rushed in. Together, we carried Manu into the hallway. Bholu splashed water on his face until he stirred back to consciousness.

Then, breathless, I hurried back towards Ashi's room.

As I passed Manu's father's room, I froze. For a split second, I saw it clearly: a human body hanging from the ceiling, eyes wide open, staring at me.

I stopped, trembling, and looked again. But the room was empty. Still, I knew—this was the second sign. They were here.

When I re-entered my room, a violent gust of wind, icy and hostile, swept past me before vanishing into the night. At that instant, the electricity returned. The lights flickered back on.

It was nearly dawn. I was overcome with exhaustion and staggered back to the hallway. The three of us lay down on the floor, drained, and finally slipped into a deep sleep.

The next morning, before I left, I told Manu, 'You were right. There are certain paranormal energies present in this Haveli. Perhaps they are demonic, perhaps harmful. But remember, I am a paranormal investigator, not a tantric baba. I can confirm that yes, they exist—but I do not have a perfect solution for you.'

Manu asked anxiously, 'What should we do now?'

I felt a subtle, almost brotherly, attachment to him, so I replied, 'Manu, I suggest you keep Ashi and your Baba alive in your happy memories. Pray for them, so their spirits can detach from the mortal world and from this Haveli. May they rest in peace. Only true love can overcome all the negative energies. They were, and always will be, your loved ones. Cast away your fears and remember them each day, even if only for a few minutes of silence. Feel comforted that they will always remain in your hearts.'

I paused, then added, 'One more thing, please keep all their belongings away from yourself and your Maa. Keep them in their respective rooms and seal those doors—forever.'

Manu's anxious eyes stayed fixed on me as I continued, 'This detachment will allow the remnants of their spirits to leave this mortal world. I sincerely hope this will help solve your problems. I truly believe that love and faith in positivity can remove demonic influences and purge negativity. Remember, the paranormal world coexists with the mortal world, and the unexplained energy that creates life is what guides us all. This world is for everyone to cherish through love and compassion.'

Manu clasped my hands with brotherly warmth and said softly, 'Jay, thank you for everything…'

My cab arrived soon afterwards. I bade him farewell and boarded it. As the car began to move, I looked back one last time. The Haveli loomed like a mammoth monster, its belly still swollen with mysteries. I closed my eyes and made a wish.

I hoped Manu and his Maa would be safe. I had told him many things—but there was something I hadn't. That secret remained caged within my own mind and soul.

8 Months Later

The Phone Call

I was sitting at my desk, reflecting on my journey. The life of a paranormal investigator is never easy. Yet it comes with a bouquet of unique experiences, and the fulfilment it brings to the heart is enormous.

My thoughts were interrupted by a phone call. I picked it up and heard a familiar voice on the other end: 'Hi Jay, how are you? This is Manu!'

The energy in his voice carried a wave of positivity. Manu continued, 'Thanks to your guidance and unforgettable help. I followed everything you told me. Now, I am happy and relieved—the hauntings have ceased completely. Perhaps the souls of Ashi and Baba are finally at peace. Maa is happy too. And there's more good news—I'm getting married next month! Thank you for everything, Jay. I will never forget you.'

I congratulated Manu. I was truly happy for him. Yet, as he spoke, the image of the Haveli flashed before my eyes. And once again, there was something I didn't tell him. That secret remained caged within my own mind and soul.

Deep in my subconscious, my intuition whispered: the demonic entity that claimed Ashi's life—and Baba's—still existed. Perhaps it was dormant now, subdued for some unforeseen reason. But my conviction told me one thing with certainty: *It will return with something ghastly—once more—someday.*

8

Angels and Demons

'When the demon came to conquer,
the angels fell like thunder.'

17 June 2019, Pari Tibba, Mussoorie, 12.55 a.m.

The 'Devil's Eye' Flares Up

The monsoons were still a month away, but the night was nothing short of horrific. Far from the hustle and bustle of the Mussoorie Hills, the atmosphere on the hilltop felt like the gateway to hell itself. A thick shroud of darkness blanketed the landscape, while gusts of wind tore through the trees and bushes, whipping up a cacophony of howls. With no human soul around, the eerie blend of silence and those chilling cries made the night feel alive—and hostile.

I sat on the wet grass, the cold biting through my clothes. My motorbike was parked over a kilometre away, and there I was—alone, at Pari Tibba, in the dead of night.

And then catastrophe struck.

Like an advancing army of shadows, dark clouds gathered in the sky, and lightning began to flash across the heavens. I had no fear of confronting the paranormal. But this wasn't the supernatural—it was nature's fury itself. One bolt of lightning could turn me to ashes in an instant. The charred remains of the massive oak tree nearby stood as a grim reminder of what the storm could do.

I got to my feet, ready to leave, when I heard them—ghastly sounds cutting through the wind. Footsteps—fast and heavy. Someone was racing towards me.

For a brief moment, a long-forgotten warning delivered to me in a deep baritone voice echoed in my mind: *'The demon descends to capture the angels and steal away the mortal souls!'*

'Rubbish!' I muttered to myself—only to realize that my five-cell electronic flashlight had gone dead. Its bulb had stopped working altogether. The faint glow of my mobile phone's flashlight wouldn't last long, and I needed to save its battery for emergencies.

The ruins of the old stone mansion around me were in terrible shape, all crumbling walls and jagged edges. My instincts screamed danger. Even though my eyes had adjusted to the dark, the shadows seemed to grow deeper, heavier.

Then, in the western corner of the ruins, I saw them.

A pair of glowing orbs.

Were they the eyes of some wild animal? Two pieces of smouldering charcoal? No…they were too big. Too alive. There was something unnatural about them, something evil simmering beneath their glow.

The burning eyes stared at me like a predator locking onto its prey. And I stood there, feeling utterly helpless, clutching my only weapon—my heavy, useless flashlight.

10 Days Ago, New Delhi

The Uncanny Messenger Calls

It was a lazy Friday evening after an exhausting week at work. I was sitting on my couch, sipping a steaming cup of coffee, when the shrill ring of my phone shattered the silence.

I answered the phone. A firm male voice on the other end asked, 'Are you Mr Jay Alani?'

'Yes, speaking.'

'Sir, my name is Tarun Baraskar. I'm calling from Mussoorie. I want to inform you about a case of fresh hauntings here. Pari Tibba—the hilltop near Landour which was once an infamous haunted spot—has long been a destination for trekkers and young couples despite its tragic legend. Years ago, two lovers were said to have been struck by lightning on top of that hill, and for decades, people claimed to see their spirits wandering the place. Over time, the legend faded, dismissed as folklore. But now...' Tarun paused for breath before continuing. 'Something has stirred it back to life. A young boy named Sunil, just 19, has become the latest victim of what people believe to be the ancient curse of Pari Tibba. His family is keeping things quiet because of the social stigma, but I've been investigating on my own. I have a lot to share with you, Sir. It feels as if the demon has returned to capture the angels.'

I was taken aback by the sheer flood of information. After a moment, I asked, 'All right. Thank you, Tarun. But tell me—what exactly do you do, and how can I help?'

'Sir,' he said, his voice tinged with worry. 'I'm an independent journalist. I've been following this case for the past two days out of personal concern for Sunil and his family.

He's much younger than me, but we went to the same college. I first met him during a college event—a bright, cheerful boy. We stayed in touch, and in a place as small as Mussoorie, our paths often crossed. To me, he's like a younger brother. And now, seeing him like this… I feel helpless.'

'Tell me everything, Tarun,' I urged. 'I need to know more before I can figure out what to do.'

'Two days ago, Sunil visited Pari Tibba. Around the same time, a tantric known as Kaapali Baba arrived in town and set up camp near the woods around Dhobi Ghat. I have reason to believe Sunil had some contact with him, though I haven't seen it myself.

'That night, Sunil was found unconscious near Pari Tibba. When I rushed to his house, his family was hostile at first, refusing to let me in. Eventually, after much pleading, I met him. He was muttering nonsense, clearly in shock. His father begged me not to spread the news. But seeing Sunil's condition, I promised to seek help.

'The police don't know anything yet. No one knows exactly what happened that night. But this Kaapali Baba has started spreading tales about angels and demons. Despite being an outsider, his words are gaining traction among the locals.

'But my concern is Sunil. He isn't recovering, and somehow, what Kaapali Baba says seems to be connected to his state. Sir, I beg you—please come and help us.'

I carefully listened to Tarun. Something in his words struck a chord with me. There was a strange pull to this case, as if it were calling me. Within moments, I made up my mind. 'Tarun,' I said firmly, 'I'll come. Give me a few days, and I'll be in Mussoorie.'

After we hung up, the questions kept swirling in my mind.

From the call, I gathered that Sunil was a perfectly normal boy. What could have terrified him so badly? He had no history of mental illness or paranormal encounters. Why had he gone to Pari Tibba that night? Who led him there? What role did Kaapali Baba play? And most importantly—what really happened on that hilltop?

There was only one way to find out.

The answers waited at Pari Tibba.

Mid-May 2019, New Delhi

The Reckless Yearning of the 'Paranormal Boy'

Even though I had been steadily working to promote my vision of paranormal reality and fight blind faith, the journey refused to become any easier with time. Priyanka was my anchor. Her presence kept me from losing myself completely to the chaos inside my mind. The dangerous combination of ambition and obsession can be a volatile one. My obsession with the paranormal was growing beyond what I could control, taking a toll on me both emotionally and physically. I always bottled up my feelings, never sharing what I went through during my investigations—but this time was different. This time, I opened up to Priyanka.

With her calm, thoughtful advice, she helped me see the truth: my work needed to remain exactly that—work. It could not be allowed to consume me as a personal mania.

As I sat beside her that scorching Sunday afternoon, confused and restless, she spoke gently yet firmly: 'Jay, focus on the positive side of what you're doing.' She added,

'If you get emotionally overwhelmed, how will you lead this crusade forward? The incident with Manu and Ashi has clearly left its mark on you. And with the volatile nature of this profession in our country—not to mention your regular work commitments—you can't afford to lose your emotional strength. If you let yourself weaken, the negativity will swallow you whole.'

I understood what she was trying to tell me. I took her hands in mine and said softly, 'I won't let the demon consume the angels within me. The strength of the Paranormal Boy must build a fortress around the reckless heart of Jay Alani, so he can keep moving forward.'

15 June 2019, Mussoorie

The Curious Case of Angels and Demons

I reached Mussoorie and checked into the hotel, where Tarun was waiting anxiously. After freshening up, I met him, feeling more composed than before. The towering Himalayas surrounding the town made everything seem vast—mysterious even.

My inner voice whispered: '*Your mission is your strength. You are stronger than ever now.*'

Our first stop was Sunil's residence. I wanted to meet him in person. Within 10 minutes, Tarun and I arrived at the house—a modest ancestral home belonging to a middle-class family.

Sunil lived there with his parents and younger sister. His father Mr Paresh, a man well past his youth, was the family's sole breadwinner. A clerk at the local government office, he carried himself cautiously, like someone who had spent his life guarding his family's safety and reputation.

I understood his hesitation. I introduced myself in the simplest possible way, careful not to alarm him further. Sunil's mother struck me as the typical homemaker—timid, overworked, and weighed down by household duties and her son's deteriorating health. But it was his sister Roshnai who caught my attention. Young, sharp-eyed and intelligent, she seemed far more perceptive than the rest. Something told me she might hold the pieces of the puzzle that we needed.

After some initial hesitation, Mr Paresh allowed me to see his son. Before I entered, he held my hand and said quietly, 'Sir, my son is young and sensitive. I don't know what happened that night, but he's been in shock ever since. The doctor—a close friend—has been treating him, but nothing seems to work. We haven't told anyone about this incident. Please…keep this within the family.'

I gave him a reassuring nod and stepped into the room.

The place was dimly lit, sunlight streaming weakly through a single window. For the first time, I saw Sunil—a lanky 19-year-old, pale and frail from the trauma he had endured. He lay slumped on the bed, his expression vacant, as though trapped somewhere between the real and the unreal.

I pulled up a chair beside him. 'Hello, Sunil,' I said gently. 'I'm Jay Alani, a paranormal investigator. I've come to help you.'

I told him everything Tarun had shared with me, speaking slowly, watching his face for any reaction. He listened in silence, his eyes blank but strangely intense, as though staring straight through me. And then, without any warning, he grabbed my hand with trembling fingers and let out a chilling cry: 'Those RED eyes! Oh God, they were ghastly! Save me! Those red, glowing eyes! They'll burn me! They were the eyes…of the DEMON himself!'

Before I could calm him down, the family rushed into the room. Sunil collapsed back into his trance, trembling violently.

I stepped out quietly, turning to the others. 'I'll get to the bottom of this,' I said.

17 June 2019, Pari Tibba, Mussoorie, 5.05 p.m.

The Road Trip

The last two days were a whirlwind, a relentless chase for answers. Though I uncovered several truths, the most crucial question remained unresolved. And so I set out towards the one place that had witnessed everything—Sunil's ordeal, the whispers of the angels, and the shadow of the demon.

With Tarun's help, I managed to rent a motorbike. It would give me the freedom to explore on my own—and the privacy I needed to meet the mysterious tantric without dragging anyone else into danger.

The investigation so far had been fruitful, but one elusive layer of this mystery remained hidden, like a locked door refusing to open.

Before leaving, I told Tarun firmly, 'If I don't return by five o'clock in the morning, come looking for me. It'll mean I'm in trouble. But don't come before then—it might ruin everything.'

I rode through the winding mountain roads, past Landour Bazaar, then Woodstock School. Beyond that, Pari Tibba lay only a few kilometres ahead. At Dhobi Ghat, just before the small village of Dhobi Gaon, I slowed down, carefully scanning the area. In the distance, I spotted the thatched hut belonging to Kaapali Baba. My helmet hid my face well enough—I was certain he wouldn't recognize me.

Without any hesitation, I followed the narrow, twisting trail leading up the hillside until I reached a three-way junction. A weathered sign pointed towards Pari Tibba. I parked the motorbike nearby and continued on foot. The air grew colder, with sudden wisps of mist that drifted in and vanished like ghosts. The steep climb over jagged rocks ended abruptly at the summit of Pari Tibba.

I stood there, surrounded by thick groves of oak and deodar. A mid-sized forest sprawled across the hilltop, broken occasionally by the remnants of old British structures.

'So this is Witch's Hill,' I whispered under my breath.

The sun was already drooping behind the mountains. Dusk would fall fast here, I knew. I checked my watch, quickened my pace, and headed straight towards my destination.

After 10 minutes of careful navigation, I found myself standing before the ruins—the crumbling stone walls beside the blackened remains of the ancient oak tree.

'This is where the demon comes to capture the Angels,' I whispered to myself.

2 Days Ago

A Bizarre 'Tantric Baba' and His Plan to Capture the Demon

As I stepped out of Sunil's house, Tarun's anxious eyes met mine. I understood his worry and said firmly, 'Have faith. I'll do everything I can. Sunil will recover—but to make that happen, I need to dig deeper into this. First, help me rent a motorbike. Then tell me where I can find Kaapali Baba.'

'Done,' Tarun replied quickly. 'I'll take you to the garage so you can rent the bike, then I'll guide you to his shack. It's between Dhobi Ghat and Dhobi Gaon Village.'

'No,' I interrupted. 'Help me rent the bike, but I'll handle the rest alone. I don't want you involved in whatever lies ahead. I have GPS—I can find him myself. Meet me at the hotel tomorrow morning.'

Within two hours, I was riding through Mussoorie's winding roads, gathering information from locals. After a brief stop near Sunil's house, I finally reached Kaapali Baba's shack. The ramshackle hut radiated a strange, hostile energy. Even before stepping inside, I could feel a wave of unease creeping over me.

Inside, by the dim glow of burning wood, sat Kaapali Baba—a stout man in saffron robes, his long white beard flowed down his chest, his eyes gleamed in the flickering firelight. The air was thick with smoke and mystery.

I checked my watch. A little past seven. The sun had set, and night had drawn its heavy curtains over the hills. In the distance, wild dogs howled.

Kaapali Baba stared at me for a long moment before gesturing silently for me to sit. I obeyed him, my mind already framing the question I had come here to ask.

'Baba,' I said, steadying my voice. 'My friend recently suffered something terrible at Pari Tibba. I want the truth. Tell me everything.'

The words seemed to strike the target. Kaapali Baba leaned forward and began his tale, his voice deep, almost ritualistic: 'The vengeful demon of the legend has awakened once again. For centuries, the Angels of Love visited Pari Tibba on stormy nights, blessing true lovers who came seeking them. But the angels were not free. They were the slaves of the demon—a cruel, ancient spirit who bound their souls, using them as puppets for his dark will.

'Then one day, everything stopped. The angels vanished, freed—or so people believed—from the demon's grasp. The legend faded from memory.

'But now the angels have returned…and so has the demon. He is hunting again, determined to reclaim what once belonged to him.'

The damp air inside the shack grew heavier as he continued, 'I have come to capture this demon and free the angels. The people here don't understand my mission, but one day they will. One day, I will trap him and peace will return to these hills. But this boy—Sunil—ignored my warnings. He went to Pari Tibba on his own.'

Kaapali Baba's eyes gleamed as he delivered the final blow. 'The demon has taken his soul. Just as he took the angels.'

A chill ran through me as he added, voice lowered to a near-growl: 'Unless I capture the Demon, the boy will never be free.'

He paused, staring at me intently, then said, 'You don't believe me. I can see it in your eyes.'

'Baba,' I replied evenly, 'this isn't about belief. It's about saving an innocent boy. That's my only duty.'

I rose, offered him a curt nod, and stepped out into the night.

As I reached my motorbike, something made me glance back. There, framed by the firelight in the doorway, stood Kaapali Baba—his eyes glowing like twin embers in the darkness, like the very demon he spoke of. A surge of defiance rose within me, and I shouted into the night, 'I will go to Pari Tibba. I will confront the demon—and the angels!'

17 June 2019, Pari Tibba, Mussoorie, 1.25 a.m.

The Zenith

I hurled the five-cell flashlight at those two blazing red eyes, and leapt out from within the crumbling stone walls. The sudden assault, followed by my quick escape, bought me a few precious seconds. I scrambled to my feet, heart pounding, ready to make my next move.

But then the noises began.

At first, they were faint—scattered footsteps, perhaps—but quickly grew in volume until it felt like the ground itself was alive. My instincts screamed: '*Either a frenzied mob is rushing towards you…or the footsteps of men have turned into the pounding of wild beasts.*'

In the dead of night, the danger confronting me was real, but my senses were in a state of chaos. The noise came from all directions. My mind spun. For a moment, I was utterly disoriented. Then, forcing myself still, I shut my eyes. Inhaled. Exhaled.

When I opened my eyes, my gut told me which way to go.

I ran. I had to, as my motorbike was over a kilometre away. I ran down a zigzag trail through the forest, across the uneven, sloping ground, finally reaching the three-way junction where I had parked it. That was my only escape.

Behind me, the growls grew louder. The pack—whatever it was—was gaining on me.

I pushed my body beyond exhaustion. Time stretched thin. Minutes felt like hours. The cold air tore through my lungs, but I didn't dare stop.

Until the slope betrayed me.

My feet slipped on loose soil, and I tumbled down the incline. Stones slashed my arms and legs as I rolled, helpless, gathering speed until my body slammed hard against the trunk of a massive oak tree. Pain exploded across my limbs. Blood trickled down my forehead. My head spun as I staggered upright—only to freeze in horror.

They were here.

A pack of beasts—dark, hulking shapes, eyes glinting in the dim moonlight, snarls splitting the silence. And at the centre, the largest of them all…

A monstrous outline. Like a wolf. Or a wild dog.

With two glowing red eyes.

The eyes of the *demon.*

Terror rooted me to the ground. Yet, even as fear clawed through my veins, my mind whispered, '*Is this truly the demon? Or something far worse?*'

And then, before I could breathe—

CRACK!

A deafening shot split the night.

A streak of something metallic cut through the darkness

and struck the giant beast with surgical precision. The creature let out a guttural roar, staggered, then collapsed, its glowing eyes wide and frozen in shock.

A tranquillizer dart.

Perfect aim; instant paralysis.

The rest of the pack scattered into the shadows, their growls fading into the night.

The forest fell silent.

Shaken, I pulled myself to my feet, limbs trembling, head spinning.

And just as the last of my strength gave way, a fierce wind tore through the trees, scattering the clouds to reveal a pale moon. My vision blurred, the world tilted...and then a hand, strong and human, caught me before I could fall.

Tarun had arrived much earlier than I had asked. Perhaps it was his anxiety—or intuition. Whatever the reason, his timing saved me from becoming another victim of the wild beasts.

As he splashed cold water on my face, the world stopped spinning. A few minutes later, I managed to stand up, though my body still throbbed with pain from the fall. My mind, however, had cleared. That's when I noticed another man with him—a tall figure in uniform, holding a service revolver.

'This is Forest Inspector Sahay,' Tarun explained quickly. 'I had a feeling something terrible might happen tonight. So I called the forest rangers. Mr Sahay agreed to come with me. Honestly, I shudder to think what might have happened if he hadn't.'

I nodded, then said firmly, 'Tarun, take photographs of that beast. We need evidence. Sunil wasn't attacked by a demon. He was mauled by wild dogs.'

Tarun clicked pictures but shook his head. 'The Dhobi Gaon area is known for its feral dogs…but this one? I've never seen a wild dog this massive.'

Inspector Sahay inspected the unconscious animal before speaking. 'I'll alert my department immediately. These creatures are a threat to locals and tourists alike. My team will be here soon to take it away.'

'Thank you, Inspector,' I replied.

He looked at me with quiet respect. 'You're a brave man, Mr Alani. I'll also inform the police. We need to clear this entire area before another incident happens.'

As dawn crept over the hills, Tarun and Inspector Sahay first took me to the hospital for treatment, then we headed straight to Sunil.

Tarun showed him the photographs of the captured beast while I said softly, 'It wasn't a Demon, Sunil. Just wild dogs. The authorities will take care of the rest.'

For the first time since I met him, Sunil smiled faintly. He sat up slowly, the fear finally fading from his eyes.

I had asked his family to wait outside. Holding Sunil's hands, I said gently, 'Love doesn't come through magic or the blessings of angels. It comes from the heart. Have faith in that.'

When we stepped out, Mr Paresh and his family were overjoyed. Roshnai stood quietly in a corner, her eyes shining with relief. I waved to them before leaving. Some questions I left deliberately unanswered.

The case, at least on the surface, was closed.

That day, I bade farewell to Tarun, extracting from him

a promise of silence. A promise to safeguard the strange secret…for Kaapali Baba had vanished from Mussoorie ever since that ill-fated night.

On my way back, a familiar unease gripped me. My inner voice rose again, whispering the questions I had been avoiding: did those red, glowing eyes belong to the wild dog, or to Kaapali Baba? How could their glares have been so eerily alike? Was there, after all, something truly *paranormal* behind it all?

I paused, drew in a deep breath, and answered myself silently: *'The line between the mortal and the paranormal worlds is like a veil of muslin—thin, fragile, almost invisible. It is best left undisturbed.'*

And in this case, I chose to bury all my lingering superstitious thoughts.

The questions I didn't ask were no longer questions to me. After meeting both Sunil and Kaapali Baba, I had secretly spoken to Roshnai. From her, I learnt about Sunil's love for a classmate named Manisha. Slowly, the pieces fell into place. Kaapali Baba had baited Sunil to visit Pari Tibba on that fateful night, luring him into danger. Perhaps he had planned similar traps for other young hearts too.

It seemed clear now—Kaapali Baba's motive was to build himself a reputation, to make the masses believe he alone could capture the so-called demon haunting the hills. Once fear gripped the locals, they would revere him. The wild dogs, I suspected, were his weapon to spread terror, though how he controlled them remained a mystery.

But destiny had other plans for me.

The last question would remain unanswered forever. My mission, however, to break the shackles of blind faith, was complete—and that was enough for me.

Perhaps, on that dreadful night atop Pari Tibba, the angels had indeed blessed us.

Or maybe it was just the hand of chance, a stroke of luck delivered by Mother Nature herself.

Who knows?

9

Man-Made Divinity

'Divinity is created by belief.
Humanity keeps it alive.'

2 December 2019, Pali–Jodhpur Highway, Rajasthan, 12.05 a.m.

The Song of the Sage

'Om Banna Dhaam! Yes, this is the divine abode of Om Banna. He spends his eternal life here, protecting both locals and travellers,' came the sombre voice of the old recluse.

His frail body, bent under the weight of age, was draped in saffron robes. An unkempt beard framed his weathered face as he sat cross-legged before me. The lone flame of an earthen oil lamp cast trembling shadows across his features, glinting in the deep hollows of his eyes before dancing on his pupils like restless fireflies.

'Om Banna left his mortal body three decades ago,' the old man continued in a voice that cracked yet carried conviction. 'But his spirit remains—a guardian angel for every pilgrim who comes here. His love for his favourite Bullet motorcycle was unbreakable. When destiny brought a tragic end to his human life, his soul chose to dwell within that very machine—a silent witness to countless miracles.'

He leaned closer, eyes gleaming in the lamplight. 'Many have seen it. The old motorcycle rides down the road on its own, engine dead, tank empty…and yet it moves. Om Banna was, is, and will always be here.'

Slowly, the recluse raised a bony hand and pointed outward. His skeletal fingers guided my gaze towards a spot in the darkness. There, encased in glass, stood the broken Bullet motorcycle, its frame draped with marigold garlands.

Moonlight spilled through the mist that clung to Pali–Jodhpur Highway. The air was cold, sharp and still. Yet the faint glow that bathed the consecrated motorcycle lent it an aura that was both sacred and unsettling—like something alive watching silently from the shadows.

15 January 2020, Recording Studio, New Delhi, 3.15 p.m.

'Gaana Podcast'

I sat in front of the mic, lost in thought. So much had happened in just a month—it felt like a rollercoaster ride I hadn't signed up for. As I closed my eyes and looked back, I realized these weren't just events. These were life-changing moments.

I knew I had to speak my heart out today. There was a storm inside me that needed to be let out—words waiting to escape into the world. I didn't know what I would cut out later while editing the episode, but one thing was certain: I had to tell this story.

I leaned closer to the mic and began:

Tonight's episode isn't just about the paranormal. It isn't just about eradicating blind faith. It isn't even just about ghosts—bhoot, as we call them in Hindi. Tonight, we talk about role models. About heroes. About how larger-than-life stories can sometimes be scarier than the ghosts we fear.

Who are these divine heroes? How do they influence society? How do they plant their beliefs deep into the minds of millions? History has seen this happen, we see it even today, and it will keep happening in the future.

Have you ever sat alone—at home, in your office—and wondered who your real role models are? Are they truly the heroes we believe them to be? Or are they leading us down a path of disillusionment? Are we all making the same mistake—blindly following the wrong idols?

I paused for a moment, then continued:

Yes, the real question is this—what is truly divine? And who defines divinity? In a world where human identity is often shaped by faith, choosing the right path becomes essential.

I introduced myself, as always:

I, Jay Alani, respect every religion, every God, every ghost, every faith, and every creed. I'm not against anything created by nature. This podcast focuses on the paranormal and the dangers of blind faith—its myths, its propaganda and its power to mislead people. Over the years, you've trusted my work, and I've stayed committed to exploring the paranormal and fighting superstition. But now it's time to question the myths that become beliefs...beliefs that turn into faith, and faith that can sometimes lead to fanaticism.

I let my words sink in before saying:

Today, we talk about one such story—a story so powerful it created its own religion. A story so extraordinary it turned a man into a god. Yes, I'm talking about the Om Banna Shrine… the shrine of Om Singh Rathod, better known as 'Bullet Baba'.

Some of you may have heard of it. For those who haven't, let me tell you this: in Rajasthan, near the village of Chotila in Pali district, there stands a shrine dedicated to a man named Om Singh Rathod, fondly called Banna, a respectful title meaning 'elder brother'.

Thousands of devotees visit the shrine of Bullet Baba every single day to seek blessings and safety on their journeys. But how did this all begin?

I leaned forward, my voice lowering as though to draw the listeners closer.

In 1988, Om Singh Rathod was riding his beloved Bullet motorcycle along Jodhpur-Pali Highway when tragedy struck. A sudden mechanical failure sent him crashing into a tree. He died instantly. The next morning, the villagers discovered the site of the accident, and news spread quickly.

Om Banna wasn't an ordinary man. He was the son of Raja Jog Singh Rathod, and heir to a royal family. His death shocked the entire region. The police investigated the accident, and cited his loss of balance as the cause of the accident. They took the damaged motorcycle to the station for safekeeping.

But then the extraordinary happened.

The next morning, the same motorcycle was found back at the crash site—under the very same tree. No one knew how it got there. The police brought it back, emptied the fuel tank, locked it securely. Yet by dawn, it was back at the accident spot once again. This happened repeatedly until fear and superstition took hold of the villagers. They believed Om Banna's spirit was tied to his beloved Bullet, returning to the place where his life ended. The locals begged the authorities to leave the motorcycle under that tree.

I paused, letting the suspense grow.

And then came another twist. Om Banna's grieving grandmother dreamt of his spirit asking her to build a shrine at the crash site so that his soul—and his motorcycle—could be remembered forever.

That was the how the Bullet Baba shrine came into being.

What began as a tragic accident soon turned into legend. Locals claimed his spirit rode the motorcycle at night, protecting travellers from harm. Pilgrims started flocking to the site, believing it would safeguard them from accidents. Over time, Om Banna wasn't just a man anymore—he became a divinity.

I ended my segment with these words:

'As I heard this incredible story, I knew I had to visit the place myself. Because sometimes, the line between myth and reality blurs in ways you cannot imagine. And this was one of those stories.'

Flashback: 2 Months Ago, New Delhi, 11.10 a.m.

A Heart-Breaking Betrayal

Delhi is always cold in November, but the November of 2019 carried a chill that seeped into my bones, freezing me in ways that went beyond the weather.

I'm Jay Alani—the paranormal investigator.

By then, my podcast with HubHopper had begun gaining real traction. The views were climbing into the millions, and people were finally recognizing the work I put into it. Yet, financially things were far from stable. The podcast brought me recognition, yes, but not enough of it to sustain me. My regular job was still my lifeline.

After two successful seasons, I was ready for more. I wanted Season 3 to be bigger, bolder, and worth every risk I had taken so far. Because in my line of work, ghosts aren't the real danger. The real danger is the venom of snakes slithering in abandoned ruins, the sting of scorpions lurking in the dark, and the sheer unpredictability of human nature. But I was stubborn. I wanted to dig deeper, go further, and give my listeners stories that would shake them to the core.

That day, I walked into the HubHopper office with my proposal for the third season. The numbers, the reach, the response—all of it spoke for itself. I was confident this was my moment.

As the promoter skimmed through the proposal, I said, 'I'm certain Season 3 will be even more successful. But I have one request. I'm a content creator, yes, but unlike many others who work in studios or behind laptops, I face real dangers while investigating these cases. My work requires time and travel, and often involves risks to life and limb. Like every creator, I need financial support. So can I expect some remuneration this time?'

Their reply hit me like a punch to the gut.

'Jay, we appreciate your work,' the promoter said. 'But unfortunately, the contract terms will remain the same. We won't be able to pay you for Season 3 either.'

For a moment, I just stood there. Then, with a calm face but a storm raging inside me, I smiled, thanked them, and walked out. By the time I left that office, I had already decided—I wasn't going to renew the contract.

On the taxi ride home, my mind was all hazy. Hunger hit me first, then exhaustion. I ate whatever I could find in the fridge, then collapsed on my bed.

As I drifted into a restless sleep, my inner voice whispered, '*So Jay Alani…you're back at square one. Start again—or perish under the weight of your own demons.*'

Three hours later, a phone call woke me up. I had left it on silent, and there were several missed calls from an unknown number. Curious, I called back.

'Hi, Jay. How are you?' said a warm, feminine voice.

I greeted her back, still groggy. 'Who's this?'

'I'm Muskaan from Gaana.com,' she said cheerfully. 'We'd love to collaborate with you. We've been following your work, and we want to bring your investigations to our platform.'

I sat up straight. 'And, will this be a paid collaboration?'

She laughed. 'Of course, Jay! It's a fully paid partnership. Can you come to our office tomorrow to discuss the details? We'd love to get started right away.'

I couldn't explain what I felt in that moment. Relief? Joy? A sense of divine timing? Maybe even something paranormal? I didn't know.

All I knew was that the heartbreak of the morning had been replaced by something extraordinary.

The very next day, I signed a stellar contract with Gaana.com. And with that, a new chapter began—a chance to refocus, to unearth bigger, bolder cases, and to tell stories that mattered.

15 January 2020, Recording Studio, New Delhi, 3.55 p.m.

'Gaana Podcast'

Unfortunately, in this country, blind faith has mushroomed across religions and regions, spreading like wildfire. In the name of spirituality, we have created countless shrines to satisfy our personal desires. Take the so-called Visa God phenomenon, for instance—people throng temples believing that offering prayers will ensure that their visa applications get approved. Isn't this turning god and spirituality into a marketplace for human ambitions? Aren't we, in the process, breeding the demons of blind faith?

The Om Banna pilgrimage—locally called the Om Banna Dhaam—is growing at an astonishing rate and is soon to come under the official administration of the Om Banna Trust. But don't we already have enough such extravagant shrines across India? Isn't this something that should worry us?

Our country is slowly becoming a manufacturing hub for man-made gods. But has anyone stopped to consider what this does to our society?

Questions. Answers. More questions. The threads of faith, fear and emotion are way too tangled for anyone to unravel them without tearing hearts apart.

2 December 2019, Fast Forward, 02.55 a.m.

At the Shrine of Bullet Baba

Almost a decade ago, as a curious teenager, I had first visited this shrine, drawn by the legend of a phantom motorcycle that supposedly rode on its own. Back then, it was a modest place with only a handful of devotees.

But this time, when I returned to the Om Banna shrine, I was stunned. The site had transformed into a sprawling complex with hotels, restaurants and shops surrounding it. The tree where Om Banna had met his tragic end was now adorned with bangles, scarves and flowers. The motorcycle itself was buried under layers of marigold garlands. I stood there silently, overwhelmed.

By evening, I found myself at a small roadside shack close by, watching the spectacle unfold. As dusk settled, a man—likely a driver waiting for his passengers who were offering prayers at the shrine—ordered tea and biscuits. Before sipping his tea, he touched his ears, bowed toward the motorcycle, and closed his eyes in reverence.

My mind wondered about his gesture. Was it faith—or blind faith? Devotion—or fear? Sincere belief—or mere habit?

I had no answers.

Moments later, a shopkeeper quietly slipped the driver some currency notes. It was clear: drivers who brought tourists to specific shops were paid a commission. Thus even in a place like this, faith was being rapidly commercialized.

When I spoke to the driver, he confirmed that he was ferrying a group of tourists to Jodhpur and they had stopped to pay homage to Om Banna.

I asked him cautiously, 'Do you really believe Om Banna's spirit lives in that motorcycle? That the stories are true?'

He looked at me earnestly. 'Sahib, Om Banna Bhagwan is real! Many have seen his phantom motorcycle on this highway. His spirit protects travellers. Anyone who skips offering prayers here risks an accident. Even the villagers believe it.'

Fear—or belief? I couldn't tell.

Then he asked, 'Haven't you heard about the truck driver from Jodhpur?'

I shook my head, and he started telling me the story: 'A few years ago, a truck driver was hauling bricks along this highway. One evening, he saw a man by the roadside asking for a lift. He stopped and gave him a ride to Jodhpur. During the journey, the man booked a full truckload of bricks, paid an advance of ₹20,000, and asked for delivery at the same spot the next day.

'The driver arrived the next day with the bricks, but couldn't find the man. When he described him to the villagers, they pointed to a framed photo of Om Banna and revealed that the man had died years ago! The driver swore it was the same person.'

I listened silently. Maybe the story was just folklore. Maybe it wasn't. I didn't want to question his faith.

That night, I decided to stay near the shrine to investigate the legend myself. I wanted to see whether the phantom motorcycle actually came to life at midnight.

As darkness fell, the area grew deserted. An old priest, living in a small hut facing the shrine, agreed to let me stay after I offered him some money, pretending my car had broken down.

'Om Banna Bhagwan lives here,' he said gravely as we waited through the night. 'Every full moon night, his spirit protects travellers.'

I kept my recording gadgets on, scanning for any unusual energy readings. Midnight came and went. Nothing happened.

At dawn, I quietly left, thanked the sleepy priest, and drove off along Jodhpur-Pali Highway.

I hadn't prayed at the shrine.

And yet, here I was—alive.

15 January 2020, Recording Studio, Delhi, 4.50 p.m.

'Gaana Podcast'

Not everything that looks terrifying is paranormal. Not every ghostly figure is the work of a supernatural force. Sometimes, acts of blind faith are far scarier. At times, the shadow of divinity itself can give birth to a world of the uncanny.

Today's case wasn't about confronting a ghost. It was about something deeper—a personal mission, a mark of the social responsibility I feel as a paranormal investigator.

I, Jay Alani, am not here to malign anyone's faith. My fight is against the *business* of blind faith—the way superstition is packaged and sold, the way innocent people are deceived in the name of God.

I am not against gods or deities. But I am firmly against the factories that manufacture 'gods' for profit.

The line between gods and ghosts, faith and fear, is often razor-thin. Both are born from the human mind—sometimes out of hope, sometimes out of fear. We imagine divine protectors or vengeful spirits to explain the unknown, to comfort our desires or justify our fears.

I respect the shrine of Om Banna. I respect the grief of those who mourn the untimely death of Om Singh Rathod. I respect the love and devotion of those who idolize him. But I cannot support the way some people have commodified his memory—turning a tragic death into a franchise of fear and divinity, forcing every passer-by to bow down to the shrine or face his imaginary wrath.

That is not faith. That is blind faith.

So what is the truth behind the legend? Does the phantom

motorcycle truly roar to life at midnight on Jodhpur-Pali Highway? Has it ever done that?

The story claims that every year, on the night of 2 December, the Bullet starts on its own and rides down the highway without any fuel, or even a rider. If this is true, there must be witnesses—policemen, villagers, someone who saw it with their own eyes. The incident isn't ancient; surely, someone is still alive to testify to it.

I challenge everyone who is listening: stay at the shrine on the night of 2 December. Watch the highway at midnight. If the motorcycle truly rides on its own, record it. Post the video online. Let the world witness this divine miracle.

But if nothing happens—if the highway stays silent—then let us stop feeding blind faith in the name of divinity.

Because blind faith doesn't just mislead one person. It misleads generations.

So yes, I fight. I fight not against faith, but against blind faith—against myths that turn into shackles for entire communities. And I will continue this fight for as long as I live.

If my words hurt the sentiments of any devotee, especially those associated with the Om Banna shrine, I apologize. My intent is not to insult anyone's belief. My intent is to separate faith from fabrication.

As I sign off today, let me say this clearly: my goal is to uncover the truth behind paranormal realities. And maybe, just maybe, Om Banna's spirit wants the same.

10

I Ain't A Saint

'A saint is born from the ashes of his sins.
But their shadows must always be left behind.'

23 April 2020, Delhi, 12.10 a.m.

The Cold Touch of Fear

Kavita restlessly tossed in bed. For over two hours, she had been trying—and failing—to sleep.

'The lockdown has left me stranded inside this apartment,' she thought. 'And all these long, inactive hours aren't even letting me burn enough calories.'

But that night was as strange as the last few nights had been.

Inside her rented apartment in Subham Residential Complex, Mumbai, she felt it again—a sudden, unnerving realization: *'Perhaps, I'm not alone here...'*

A bleak shadow seemed to wrap itself around her—a formless, nameless presence, like an invisible blanket closing in on her by the second.

Kavita was an independent, modern and brave young woman. She worked in Mumbai, lived alone, and never gave in to superstition. But tonight, something felt wrong.

As the hands of the clock crept past midnight, she felt a shiver run down her spine. A voice—soft and cold—whispered in her ear: 'Hey, dear…hold my arms. I'm afraid…lonely. I know you're lonely too. Come…hug me. Be my friend. I live here with you, day and night…but we're still strangers.'

Kavita sat upright in bed, trembling. Beads of sweat appeared on her forehead. Her heart pounded wildly. She glanced around the room. The dim blue light of the night lamp cast long, eerie shadows.

She had never felt such terror in her life.

Swallowing hard, she tried to make sense of it.

What was that? Who was speaking? Was it a man? A woman?

She didn't know. Fear gripped her very being.

Then she heard the voice again, harsher this time—like a gust of icy wind rushing through her very bones: 'Where are you searching? I'm your only companion. I'm right beside you…inside you…all around you.'

And then it happened.

Kavita felt it—a cold, vaporous touch on her shoulder.

Like frozen fingers trailing down her arm.

She gasped silently, unable to scream. Her whole body shook as a chilling breath swept over her neck and shoulder.

The fear was too much.

A strangled moan escaped her throat—and then everything went black.

Just before she fainted, she saw it—hazy blue smoke filling the entire room, blotting out everything.

When Kavita woke up the next morning, sunlight streamed into her room. Her head throbbed. Her body felt weak. She sat up slowly, holding her head in both hands.

'Must've been a nightmare,' she whispered to herself.

But before she could even finish the thought, the voice came again—low, cold, and unmistakable: 'I'm not a dream. I'm as real as you are. And I'm your only companion now.'

30 January 2020, Patna, Bihar, 11.25 a.m.

The Letter Arrives

Mr Narayan Alani sat in his living room, sipping tea and reading the newspaper. It was a lazy Thursday morning, the winter chill still hanging in the air.

A courier arrived. Vishnu, his office peon and part-time assistant at home, brought in the package and placed it on the table.

It was an envelope.

'Open it, Vishnu,' Mr Alani said casually.

Vishnu tore it open and handed him the letter. 'Sir, there's no sender's address. Isn't that strange?'

Curious, Mr Alani took the envelope and the letter. As his eyes scanned the handwritten lines, his face changed. His eyes widened. His whole body felt numb.

The letter read:

'Shri Narayan-ji,

Whatever your son is doing is not right. He is a devil—a demon on this earth. This is not an empty threat but a serious warning. Stop him now, or we will KILL HIM.

He marches ahead on his crusade against faith and religion, deceiving people, turning them away from the Gods. He is evil inside and out.

If he isn't stopped immediately, know this—*we* will stop him. We are the holy mercenaries of the Gods, strong enough to crush such filthy creatures under our feet.

Anyone who harms the image of our Gods will face consequences that the world will never forget…'

30 January 2020, New Delhi, 1.15 p.m.

A Horrified Father

Just like every other individual in the world, I was also a victim of the pandemic. The lockdowns hadn't begun yet and the Covid-19 scare was yet to reach its peak—sporadic incidents were being reported worldwide. I was busy with the latest experiment I had undertaken. Yes, it was a Paranormal Helpline, and I was pursuing it with vigour.

As news about India's first-ever Paranormal Helpline spread across the country, slowly but steadily, I began receiving calls from people. I must admit that many of these calls were bogus. Some were prank calls, while some were abusive. However, to my relief, there was also a handful of genuine calls from people who truly needed help.

Day by day, the frequency of calls gradually increased, which made me happy. I had already started exploring other creative avenues, such as books and audio-visual formats, and I felt that my dream was finally turning into reality.

That afternoon, I was sitting at the dining table having a quiet lunch. I had taken a few days off from work and was enjoying the idle afternoon. Suddenly, the phone rang. It was Baba. It was unlike him to call me at this hour.

He came straight to the point. 'Jay, what are you up to?

At first, you wanted to do engineering but left it midway. Then you studied mass communication and joined a media company. But you left that too! Now you're into paranormal investigations with all these weird cases.' He caught his breath. 'This is totally insane! Most of these cases are beyond my comprehension and I still don't understand what exactly you do professionally! And now… Now you have invited threats from shady elements. Jay, what is happening?' I was suddenly overcome with guilt. He sounded fatigued and exasperated.

'Baba, please calm down,' I said. 'I don't want you to get agitated and fall sick.'

After a long pause, I asked, 'Now, please tell me, what's this threat you have received?'

'A letter arrived this morning—not a regular letter. It reads like a warning message for you. I fear for your safety, my son. What is going on?'

As he read out the first few lines, I interrupted him and told him to send me photos of the letter and the envelope.

I quickly read the message and skimmed through the photos Baba had sent on WhatsApp. Unfortunately, the envelope didn't have an address. By then, I was quite certain that the threat was an outcome of the 'Bullet Baba' case. Perhaps I had provoked one of his staunch devotees. Bullet Baba had been elevated to the status of a deity, and there was bound to be some outrage over my statement.

All said and done, I tried to make sense of the situation. Did Godmen like Bullet Baba exercise so much control over the masses that a mere statement from an outsider like me was enough to shake their entire belief system to the core? Is this what blind faith was all about?

Across the globe, every religion and faith has numerous people raise difficult questions about the existence of these Gods. Are these questions potent enough to shake the foundation of the faith itself?

No, dear reader, I am not a pagan—I'm not a disbeliever. I have full faith in my own religion and respect other faiths too. I strongly believe that the entire universe is governed by a Supreme Power that goes by different names in various religions. I'm not a great philosopher and I don't question the existence of God—nor do I wish to create a controversy for the sake of it. However, when I see the brutality and rigidness associated with religion—or committed on the pretext of religion—I choose to question the same and stage a protest.

Paranormal investigation is not a mere job where you flaunt fancy gadgets, proving the existence of ghosts and dismantling people's faith in a divine power. I'm a paranormal investigator as it's my crusade to eliminate blind faith among India's masses. I strongly believe that there's a vast difference between following God as opposed to following godmen. We, as members of a civilized society, must choose wisely.

After the call with Baba, I did my best to find some information about the sender. However, it was a fruitless exercise as details of the sender simply couldn't be tracked. Finally, I gave up and abandoned my efforts.

Later that day, I had a heartfelt chat with Baba to reassure him about my mission's purpose. 'Baba, this is just a prank—and there may be more in the coming days,' I warned. 'Please ignore them. You don't have to worry about my safety; I promise that I'll never do anything that would hurt your dignity and damage your trust in your son.'

By the time we wrapped up the call, I could sense the relief in his voice. He started feeling more reassured about my life's mission.

And as time passed, I started to forget about the incident.

25 April 2020, Delhi, 6.10 p.m.

The 'Ghost' in the 'Mirror'

The pandemic was an unprecedented black-swan event for the modern world. The human race as we know it came to a standstill when WHO declared Covid-19 as a worldwide pandemic.

I still remember the evening when the lockdown was announced in India. I was seated on my couch and sipping coffee after a long day at work. Covid-19 cases had spiked across the nation and a surreal fear of the virus had gripped the masses.

The lockdown announcement felt like the last nail in the coffin. I was anxious and called Baba. I wanted to hear his soothing voice.

'Jay, this is going to be a long battle. Stay calm; we're in this together— as always.' I gathered strength from Baba's words and mentally prepared myself for the solitary confinement. In the days that followed, I threw myself headlong into work— or rather, as much work as was feasible given the lockdown restrictions.

Although I was unable to continue physical excavations and investigations, I now had the time to execute my passion project that had been in the works for a while.

The Paranormal Helpline was now active and amidst the lockdown blues, I tried to feel enthusiastic about helping people who might need my guidance.

In the ensuing weeks, the Paranormal Helpline was inundated with calls and I was totally overwhelmed by the sheer volume of it! At one point, I received as many as 200 calls a day! No kidding.

Eventually I had to disable the helpline's calling feature as it was taking a toll on my physical and mental health.

I was the sole person answering the calls, and there was no fancy call centre to assist me. What's more, several of them turned out to be prank callers. I enabled the messaging feature to ensure genuine people could still reach out to me if they were in dire need of help.

The decision was good and I felt much better. I even chose to respond to messages on my Facebook or Instagram accounts. It made me happy that I could still engage with my audience without losing my sanity during a time of global upheaval.

One evening, I received a DM on Instagram. It was from a girl named Kavita. The message read, 'Jay, I need your help immediately!'

I replied, 'How can I help you?'

'Please help me. I need to talk to you right away! It's about a paranormal occurrence in my apartment...'

Instantly, I decided to pursue the matter as I intuitively felt a need to help the woman. Something drove me to find out about the paranormal occurrence she'd experienced.

Often, people choose to ignore such complaints, but doing so can actually prove fatal for the victim. I messaged back sharing my personal phone number. Within minutes, I heard from her.

'Hi Jay, I'm Kavita. I'm 28, living alone in a rented

apartment in Mumbai. My parents are in Bangalore, where my father runs a small business. I have a decent job, but the lockdown has left me completely marooned…'

After the initial exchange of greetings, I carefully listened to everything she said. Kavita continued, 'Jay, things have been difficult ever since the lockdown began, but recently, something unbearable has started happening. For the past week, there's been a paranormal presence in my apartment. I'm not losing my mind, nor am I saying this on a whim. It's real—a ghastly apparition has taken up residence here. It tries to befriend me, steal my soul. At first, I thought it was my imagination. But this…thing is here all day. It whispers in my ears and touches me with its cold fingers! Ooohhh… I feel so helpless. I can't even look in the mirror anymore. It stares at me through the mirror with its deathly eyes! This isn't in my head. It happened again just a few minutes ago—that's why I messaged you right away. My nerves are about to snap… I feel like I might die!'

Kavita sobbed like a child before adding, 'Jay, I don't want to die! Please do something.'

Something about her words hit me hard. I knew Kavita needed serious help—before she became the victim of something truly terrible. Deep inside, I sensed what needed to be done. I told myself: *'I know how to fight this ghost…even if I'm far away from the place and the person being haunted.'*

I finally replied to her messages: 'Kavita, whenever you feel scared or lonely, call me on this number. You can even do a video call if things get too frightening. The lockdown keeps me from coming over right now, but I promise you—within a month, this devil will be gone for good.'

12 February 2020, New Delhi, 11.45 a.m.

Inside a Dark Den

A few days passed since the incident with the letter. It was a Saturday, and I was at home skimming through my Instagram messages when suddenly a new one arrived:

'Jay Alani, you have tainted the altar of faith, religion and God. You shall now face the wrath of the mercenaries. Be ready for the consequences.'

Instantly, I knew this was my chance to get hold of the cowards who had dared send that letter to my parents. Anger simmered in me as I played along, even apologizing and pretending to be scared, hoping they'd reveal something.

The person on the other end sounded overconfident. 'Good that you understand. Last time when Baba Trilokenath threatened you, it didn't affect you. Filthy creatures like you need strong fists to destroy you.'

I silently smirked—he had unwittingly committed a blunder, and revealed the identity of the perpetrator: Baba Trilokenath.

I immediately searched online. Fake godmen thrive on publicity, and sure enough, an old Facebook post gave me the address I needed. Baba Trilokenath ran an ashram in Jaipur. That was all I needed to know. I grabbed my car keys, called a few friends, and we set off for Jaipur. It was time to end this cycle of karma.

Inside the ashram, I met Baba Trilokenath. I had paid for a private audience, so I was ushered into a separate room with him and three of his attendants. That was exactly what I wanted.

The Baba sat on a decorated cot while a creaky table-fan failed to move the stifling air. I greeted him and asked, 'Baba, do you know me?'

Much to his displeasure, I didn't touch his feet or seek his blessings.

'I'm Jay Alani.' I came straight to the point, making myself comfortable on the ragged mat on the floor. 'I'm the one you threatened in that letter you sent to my family.'

Baba Trilokenath raised his eyebrows in amusement. 'Ah, yes, I remember now.' He chuckled. 'You're the one who did that nonsense investigation on Bullet Baba, aren't you? The man trying to destroy people's faith. You media people have no spine—you'll do anything for money.'

I had no interest in arguing with the man who was clearly a fraud. I simply wanted to make it clear that seekers of truth are never cowards.

Silently, I rose to my feet. Our eyes locked.

'I have something important to tell you,' I hissed under my breath, provoking his attendants to step forward.

A feeble murmur escaped him: 'Umm…hmmm…?'

I leaned in close, my lips nearly touching his ear. 'If you ever dare threaten me or my family again, I promise you—I'll strip away this priestly disguise you wear while exploiting the faith and hard-earned money of the poor. Next time, send your warning to *my* address, not to my parents. If you want to fight, fight me directly!'

There was pin-drop silence in the room.

I added after a long pause, 'Try living like the poor labourers you cheat every day. See how tough life really is. And the next time you threaten me, you'll find out who's really powerful.'

Sweat glistened on Baba Trilokenath's forehead. He was speechless.

Without another word, I walked out. I was still livid with rage, but there was a certain pride in my stride.

In hindsight, I regret threatening him—not because he was a godman, but because anger always leaves destruction in its wake. **Perhaps I should have forgiven him, but I ain't a saint.**

10 May 2020, Delhi, 8.30 p.m.

Paranormal or a New Normal?

In the past 15 days, I made a new friend—Kavita. No, it wasn't because I was lonely or looking for company. I needed to travel to Mumbai, to her apartment, and meet her in person. I had to investigate further into the apparition that was bothering her. But the pandemic and the lockdown made that impossible. So I came up with a different plan: Kavita would become my eyes and ears, and I would be hers.

It sounds complicated, but in simple terms, I decided to be her constant, albeit remote, companion during those long and difficult days.

We spoke for hours, and slowly, I could sense her fear ebbing away. At first, she was reserved—always polite, with a quiet dignity that matched her modern values and impeccable manners. She was beautiful—both inside and out—graceful, elegant and composed. Over time, she began to open up, telling me about her childhood, her parents, her friends, her school days and college life. She spoke of the bullies she had faced, the jealousies she had overcome as she climbed the ladder of success at work.

Kavita was a strong woman. But life had dealt her a cruel hand.

She told me about the boy she had once loved and the painful betrayal that ended it all during the lockdown.

'I even tried to call him several times,' she said bitterly. 'But he was as cold as a corpse! Jay, I didn't break down, though. With an iron fist, I shut that chapter of my life. A few days ago, he tried calling me again, sent messages. I've blocked him. There's no space in my heart for betrayers.'

As it happened, the apparition in her apartment still haunted her. Whenever it returned, she would call me and I would interrogate her about its presence to understand the phenomenon better. As the days passed, the apparition's visits became less frequent, and slowly, Kavita began to heal. But one fear lingered—she still couldn't look into the mirror at night. The terror of facing whatever lurked there had gripped her.

One night, I decided to do something drastic.

'Kavita,' I said over the phone. 'I want you to do something for me. Let's switch to a video call. Don't be scared. Nothing bad will happen—I promise.'

She hesitated at first but agreed.

When the call connected, I said, 'Now switch to the back camera on your phone and follow my instructions carefully.'

Her face betrayed a flicker of anxiety.

'Don't worry,' I reassured her. 'Go to the mirror on your dressing table. Point the camera at it.'

A little shaken by the sudden request, she obeyed. She stood before the large mirror, her reflection filling the screen.

Her shoulders were tense, her eyes downcast. She couldn't bring herself to look into the mirror.

I watched the reflection in silence, sensing her mounting fear.

'Jay…what next?' she asked nervously. 'Are you there? What do I do now?'

'Look up,' I said, my voice firm. 'Look straight into the mirror.'

She raised her eyes and looked into the mirror.

One second. Two. Three. Five.

And then she screamed. 'It's gone! Jay, the ghost is gone!'

I smiled. 'Yes, it's gone. And I promise you—it will never return.'

Her eyes widened. 'But how? How did you do it?' she asked, almost in tears, and the relief on her face was palpable.

'Kavita,' I said gently, 'there *was* a ghost in your house—your own ghost. It was the ghost of your loneliness, haunting you through that mirror. Tonight, you conquered it with your own strength. I had my suspicions about the "apparition" for a while, but wanted to put it to test before confirming whether this was indeed the case.'

Even in her joy, tears streamed down her face. She smiled like a child and whispered, 'Jay, thank you! Thank you so much for everything.'

25 May 2020, New Delhi, 4.50 p.m.

I Ain't a Saint

As was evidenced, Kavita was never the victim of a supernatural or paranormal entity. She was the victim of solitude and isolation. The New Normal had started to feel like an alternate 'paranormal' experience, and the dangers of that were far too real. As a committed paranormal investigator, I couldn't allow that to happen.

As the days passed, Kavita slowly adapted to the work-from-home culture. I encouraged her to watch uplifting videos online, read good books, and surround herself with positivity. We still spoke on the phone, but I deliberately reduced the frequency of our conversations. I wanted her to regain her strength and not become emotionally dependent on me to cope with the other pandemic that had gripped mankind: loneliness.

Another 15 days went by, and Kavita was back to living her life with renewed energy. Her personality, her mind, and her spirit adapted to the New Normal. The lockdown had caused chaos in her life, yes, but it also opened a door—an opportunity to start afresh, to make new friends, to look at life with hope instead of fear.

As for me—

I, Jay Alani, am not one of those so-called investigators who flaunt fancy gadgets and claim to unearth demons with grotesque faces and mutilated features. I am an honest, no-nonsense paranormal investigator who factors in a humane aspect in his investigations. I know that the ghosts born out of human fears and loneliness are often far scarier than any lingering spirit from the past which may coexist alongside us in some parallel realm.

Yes, I have always been against blind faith—and will remain so until my last breath, and perhaps even beyond death. My journey as a paranormal investigator began as a crusade against blind faith, and it continues with the same purpose.

After the pandemic ended, my mission assumed a new meaning.

I, Jay Alani—'the Paranormal Boy'—have pledged to carry this crusade forward so that people are unshackled from the chains of blind faith.

And I want to tell the world this:

Ghosts—wherever they may exist—were once humans too. Like the living world, that realm deserves respect too. The paranormal should not be mixed with superstition; it is part of the unexplained truth that shapes life itself. Being alive and being a ghost are two sides of the same coin. We live because we coexist as humanity.

My battle is not against ghosts.

My battle is not against God.

My battle is against demons—humans who perpetuate blind faith.

Demons that make people strip women of their dignity.

Demons that cause childhood abuse, leaving lifelong scars.

Demons that commit mercy killings in the name of religion.

Demons that let patients die because families choose fake healers over doctors.

This is why I fight.

To everyone reading this—to everyone who has followed the journey of the Paranormal Boy, I would like to reiterate that my battle against blind faith will continue as long as it exists in our society.

My journey has only just begun.

After the pandemic ended, my mission assumed a new meaning.

Everything—the Parliament, the courts—gave pledges. I [illegible] this crisis to create so [illegible] people are [illegible] from the chains of blind faith.

And I want to tell the world this:

Ghosts exist; they may [illegible] were once humans [illegible] the living world that [illegible] deserves [illegible]. The paranormal should not be mixed with superstition. It is part of the inexplicable [illegible] the [illegible] itself. [illegible] and people [illegible] are two sides of the same coin. We live because we coexist as humanity.

My battle is not against ghosts.

My battle is not against God.

My battle is against demons—humans who perpetuate blind faith.

Demons that make people drop [illegible] and their dignity.

Demons that chase childhood away, leaving lifelong scars.

Demons that commit merciless killings in the name of religion.

Demons that let patients die because families [illegible] over doctors.

This is why I fight.

To everyone reading this—to everyone who has followed the journey of the Paranormal Boy, I would like to [illegible] that my battle against blind faith will continue as long as it exists in our society.

My journey has only just begun.

Acknowledgements

First and foremost, we express our heartfelt gratitude to our families for being our unwavering support system. Their faith in us has been the backbone of this work.

We are deeply grateful to the team at *The Book Bakers*, one of the country's leading literary agencies, for believing in this project. Thank you for guiding our literary journey over the years and inspiring us to write a story that boldly confronts society's real evils and injustices. Suhail Mathur, your steadfast support for this manuscript—and all our work—means the world to us. We truly value our association with you and your entire team.

Our sincere appreciation goes to our dynamic publisher, Rupa Publications, for consistently supporting our work. We are especially thankful to our devoted Senior Commissioning Editor, Ms Kausalya Saptharishi, whose belief in this book has been invaluable. Her personal commitment, editorial expertise, and trust in our vision have greatly enriched this project. We also extend our gratitude to our copy editor, Ms M.D. Mahasweta, whose meticulous efforts have helped refine this manuscript to its best possible form.

The Paranormal Boy chronicles a paranormal investigator's mission to dispel blind faith and uphold human dignity. This book is for anyone curious to discover the real story of a quiet, determined crusade to challenge misconceptions about the paranormal world.

Thank you,
Jay Alani & Prasun Roy